D0549083

Space
clearing

Space
clearing

The ancient art
of purifying,
cleansing and
harmonizing
your living space

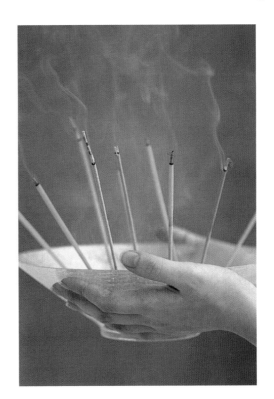

stella martin

LORENZ BOOKS

This edition is published by Lorenz Books

Lorenz Books is an imprint of Anness Publishing Ltd
Hermes House, 88–89 Blackfriars Road, London SE1 8HA
tel. 020 7401 2077; fax 020 7633 9499
www.lorenzbooks.com; info@anness.com

© Anness Publishing Ltd 2002

This edition distributed in the UK by Aurum Press Ltd
25 Bedford Avenue, London WC1B 3AT
tel. 020 7637 3225; fax 020 7580 2469

This edition distributed in the USA and Canada by
National Book Network, 4720 Boston Way, Lanham, MD 20706
tel. 301 459 3366; fax 301 459 1705; www.nbnbooks.com

This edition distributed in Australia by Pan Macmillan Australia
Level 18, St Martins Tower, 31 Market St, Sydney, NSW 2000
tel. 1300 135 113; fax 1300 135 103
customer.service@macmillan.com.au

This edition distributed in New Zealand by David Bateman Ltd
30 Tarndale Grove, Off Bush Road, Albany, Auckland
tel. (09) 415 7664; fax (09) 415 8892

All rights reserved. No part of this publication may be reproduced,
stored in a retrieval system, or transmitted in any way or by any means,
electronic, mechanical, photocopying, recording or otherwise, without
the prior written permission of the copyright holder.

A CIP catalogue record for this book is available from the British
Library.

Publisher: Joanna Lorenz
Managing Editor: Helen Sudell
Senior Editor: Joanne Rippin
Designer: Nigel Partridge
Photographer: Michelle Garrett
Production Controller: Claire Rae

With thanks to the following agencies for permission to reproduce
their images: AKG (London) p12 The Birth of Venus, Adolphe
Bouquereau, p14 Dance of the Wild Men from Froissart, p66 Druids of
the Forest, Vincenzo Bellini; The Bridgeman Art Library p68 A Fairy
Song, Arthur Rackham.

10 9 8 7 6 5 4 3 2 1

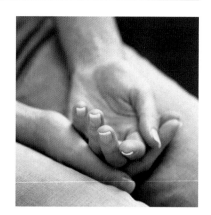

Contents

introduction

The principles of space clearing are based on the belief that all locations have a spirit of place. When acknowledged and cared for, this spirit can have a positive effect on the place and all those who occupy it. But environments can also be adversely affected by the build-up of negative vibrations. They therefore require regular clearing. Just as physical housework clears dust and debris from a home, so spiritual housework lifts the atmosphere of a place to a higher level of peace.

Our basic physical requirements are food, water and a home, yet we are more than just physical by nature. We have a strong spiritual side as well, which is manifested in such things as the universal evolution of religion and the ageless wisdom of the world's spiritual teachers. In early times it was recognized that the home was a very spiritual place. The Romans believed that each home had its resident *genius loci* – the individual deity of the place – and each household had a special altar, where at certain times the family would gather to give thanks for their security. The same idea occurs in traditional Chinese and Indian thought, and similar spiritual belief systems can be found all over the world and in all ages. In modern society, a growing awareness of the importance of sacred space is now rekindling this ancient need to sanctify our homes and environments. Space clearing is an important factor in our rediscovery of the spiritual aspect of life.

This book explores different cultural approaches to space clearing. It describes many of the ancient magical, mystical, practical and psychic sources that have long been used, and explains how we can keep our own environments clean and clear, as our ancestors once did. Its aim is to rekindle an interest in spiritual harmony in both the home and the workplace, so that everyone who enters or lives there will benefit from an atmosphere full of harmony, clarity and peace.

The Ancient Art of Space Clearing

Every human spirit requires peace and quiet,
and home is the place, above all others, where
we should be able to shut out the bustle and
anxieties of the world. The spiritual integrity of
the home was revered by our ancestors, and the
rituals they observed to protect and maintain it
hold valuable lessons for the modern world.

Spirit of place

It is one of the primal urges of animal life to seek out a location in which it can feel safe: a lair, a nest, a den, a shell, a tree or a cave. Human beings share that basic impulse with other animals, and we need to feel instinctively that we are secure.

We cannot be completely at ease in our surroundings unless our spiritual side is also comfortable. The human species may be technologically advanced, but within us there still resides a vestige of that mysterious "sixth sense" that is possessed by all creatures. We can find many instances of its influence in the natural world. There are trees, seemingly indistinguishable from others, in which no birds will nest. There are corners of a house where no cat will linger to sleep. We humans, too, receive and react to this kind of subliminal input, and throughout history there have been those who have understood this and have recognized its importance to our wellbeing.

We choose our carpets because we like their colour or pattern, but the traditional designs from the Far East, Turkey and North Africa were woven to attract good fortune and domestic tranquillity to the places in which they were laid. This tradition has roots in even older cultures: the mosaic floors of the Romans and Greeks served the same purpose. We hang pictures on our walls because we like to look at them, but their origin also lies with the murals of ancient civilizations. For the Egyptians, Minoans, Greeks and Romans, wall paintings often served a spiritual purpose in placating and invoking local deities, who would thus be more inclined to favour the dwelling with their blessing. Further back still, this kind of spiritually enhancing decoration can be seen in the prehistoric cave paintings of France and Spain and their more recent equivalents executed by the Bushmen of Africa and the native Australians.

All these devices were originally intended to drive away bad vibrations or evil spirits and attract good, harmonious ones in their place. They were for clearing negativity and encouraging good vibrations. They were for space clearing.

psychology and intuition

As humankind grew more scientific in outlook, society tended to dismiss the ways of our forebears, but now there is a growing realization that we should not divorce ourselves from our ancient spiritual heritage. An appreciation of the power of the old ways is beginning to return.

All the traditional belief systems of the world include the principle of space clearing. The tribal witch doctor is conducting space clearing when he dresses

△ We need the comfort and security of a place where we feel at home, and instinctively surround ourselves with things we hold dear.

▷ When our home environment is balanced and harmonious, it is easier to relax and unwind there.

▷ **The simplest of altars – such as an arrangement of beautiful natural objects on a windowsill – can restore the spirit.**

in a mask and feathers and dances with rattles inside a hut. Whatever we may think of his particular method, it is a means to an end, and that end is to make the occupants of the dwelling feel good about their home because something magical has been done to drive away evil spirits. We may prefer to speak of negative vibrations rather than evil spirits, but the principle remains the same.

Psychology relates to the psyche, the deepest subconscious level of the mind. If we are not feeling comfortable at a subconscious level, we may not be able to put that feeling into words; we may not even realize that we are feeling ill at ease. Nevertheless, our ability to be happy and relaxed will be subtly impaired, and our whole outlook on life is liable to be adversely affected.

Our perception of the atmosphere of a space operates at a subconscious level. The positive changes felt by those who ask the witch doctor to make a house call are certainly psychological, but this does not mean the benefits are any less real.

creating positive space

Space clearing is the art of making a home or workplace feel good as an environment in which we can live at ease and go about our daily lives. Some people, thinking in purely material terms, may believe that if they spend enough money on a house they will automatically be happy there, but experience often shows this is not the case. Most of us have visited what seems like a "perfect" residence that has been expensively decorated, only to feel somehow alienated and uncomfortable. Our psyche, or unconscious sixth sense, is at work again.

There is no doubt that some places feel cold or watchful while others, while they may not seem different in any obvious way, make us feel warm and welcome. Space clearing is the art of introducing the change from one condition to the other. It can be carried out wherever it is needed – in a

house, flat, room, office or even in a factory or workshop. It can be extended to the garden and to places we stay in temporarily when travelling, such as hotel rooms.

Today, we often hear of problems such as "sick building syndrome" and "geopathic stress". These terms are used to describe the dysfunctional energy in a place that seems to have an adverse effect on the people who live or work there. Multinational companies are fully aware of the existence of these phenomena, and employ feng shui experts or architects cognizant with sacred geometry to correct the problem and restore the free flow of their businesses.

Even though techniques like space clearing may at times have been dismissed by the "scientific" way of thought and pushed into the background of modern belief, our need for such traditions has never entirely gone away, and our lives and humanity have been impoverished whenever they are not acknowledged. Such things may be categorized by some people as superstitious magic and therefore not

worthy of serious consideration – but of how much value is a life that has no room for magic in it? It has often been said that it is impossible to draw a line between magic and psychology. Perhaps if we were to allow more magic into our lives, there would be less need for psychologists to heal our troubled minds.

▷ **Fresh flowers, plants and crystals not only bring interest and colour into an interior, but lift the atmosphere with their natural energy.**

The power of the spirits

As well as acknowledging the nameless spirits that sanctified and safeguarded a place, many traditions sought the protection and goodwill of the major deities. Symbols and depictions of gods and goddesses, and acts of devotion at the domestic altar, were a means of engaging in communication with the spiritual world. They honoured the powers that it was hoped would in turn confer blessings on the home and bring good fortune to its inhabitants. Some deities came to be particularly associated with the protection of the home, such as the Roman god Janus, who guarded the entrances, and the goddess Vesta, who presided over the hearth at the centre of domestic life.

Prayers are one method of focusing the thoughts in order to engage with the higher realm of the spirits, but there are other ways

▽ Prayer has been used in many cultures to engage with a higher realm of consciousness.

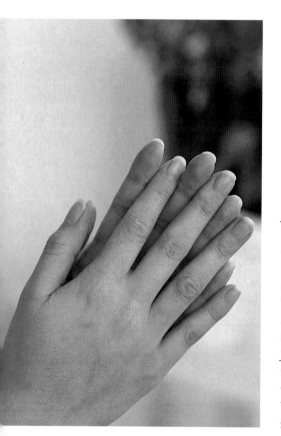

that this state of mind can be approached, such as meditation and the use of rituals and invocations. Specific scents and sounds can also serve to point the mind in a particular spiritual direction.

invoking the spirits

The higher, or astral, realms are usually described in terms that mirror human existence, because that is the only way in which we can comprehend them. It is natural that the energies of our lives should have been personified in the forms of gods and goddesses and various other spiritual entities, each of which embodies particular characteristics. In the ancient Greek pantheon, for instance, Aphrodite is recognized as the goddess of love, while Hermes is the patron of messages, healing and teaching.

Every astral entity has its own area of "speciality", and we can put ourselves in tune with that particular energy by meditating upon the astral form that personifies it. By communing with these spiritual powers we can enhance the side of our own nature that corresponds to their individual energies. This is the basis of invoking the power of the spirits. By so doing, we allow the subconscious mind to achieve communion with astral forms.

Every culture has produced its own names and ideas for picturing these entities, sometimes with sub-cultural variations. As just one example, the Anglo-Saxon sky-god Tiw (from whose name we derive Tuesday – "Tiw's day") can be identified with Tyr in Scandinavia, Tiwaz in northern Europe, Ziu in Germany and Dyaus in ancient India. The Sanskrit name Dyaus is related to the Aryan Djevs ("sky" or "light") or Deivos, and to the Greek Zeus and the Roman Jove. Likewise, the spiritual embodiment of the love-energy appears in many pantheons, with many names other than Aphrodite or Venus, and is always represented by a female form. The great psychologist Karl Jung

△ Aphrodite, the Ancient Greek goddess of love, can be invoked if you are seeking aid with an issue concerning love or the emotions. She and the other ancient gods are aspects of archetypes that are, in a sense, patterns for self-change.

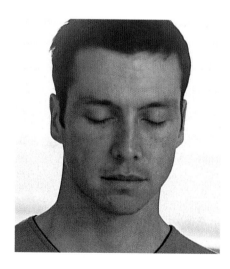

△ Everyone can benefit from taking a few moments to themselves to calm and focus their thoughts and feelings.

PROTECTIVE DEITIES

You can dedicate an altar to a protective deity such as those listed here, at any time when protection or blessings are required in your life.

Shiva, the Hindu Lord of the Cosmic Dance, and a powerful protective force for justice, healing and strength. When invoking Shiva, always light a candle to honour his presence. Serpents, elephants and the white bull are sacred to him. Use white candles on his altar.

Kali, the Hindu triple goddess and consort to Lord Shiva. She protects from all negative forces, and helps to reveal the truth. Marigolds are her sacred flower. Offerings to Kali of pleasing foods should be displayed on fresh green leaves. Use black candles on her altar.

Anubis, the ancient Egyptian jackal-headed deity and protector from psychic forces. Burn myrrh grains in a charcoal burner before a statue of Anubis or pictures of the jackal. Use indigo blue candles on his altar.

Innana, the Sumerian goddess of victory. She is highly venerated as the defender of peace, justice and the law. Lion and dog iconography can be placed on her altar, together with a wand strung with ribbons that is twirled when calling to her. Use red candles on her altar.

Hecate, the Greek goddess of the moon. She wards off evil and purifies and transforms negativity. A woven willow basket, fairy icons, dogs and frogs can be displayed. Use black candles on this altar.

Isis, the ancient Egyptian lunar goddess and protector of women. She brings healing and protection to the home. You can display a basket of figs, a small bowl of cow's milk, and hold a piece of carnelian or lapis lazuli while invoking her. Use turquoise blue candles in her honour.

called such deities archetypal beings. The power of the spirits is very real, not least because it has been reinforced by belief through the generations. By communing with them we enhance the side of our nature that corresponds with their energies.

▷ Creating time to meditate will allow your subconscious to commune with higher realms.

△ Lord Shiva, the Hindu creator deity, can be called upon whenever you are seeking transformation or clarity.

The folklore tradition

Many ancient space clearing ceremonies have persisted into the modern age as part of the folklore tradition. The spiritual beliefs and practices of our forebears gave rise to numerous local rituals that play an important part in the continuity of the community.

traditional forms of space clearing

"Beating the bounds" is an old custom whose original purpose was the spiritual protection of the community. The village boundary line was beaten with birch wands to ensure the safekeeping of the village and establish a magical barrier around it so that no evil spirit could enter. In more recent times, the ceremony also had a secondary purpose: to teach the boys who accompanied the parish officers round the village to remember the position of the boundary, as a way of averting future disputes about land ownership.

In the Basque villages of the Pyrenees, ancient carnival rites have a similar purpose. The men of Ituren and Zubieta, for

▽ Garlic is well known to have a cleansing effect on the body, but in the old days it was also believed to drive out inner demons.

example, wearing dunces' caps and sheepskins with huge sheeps' bells tied on their backs, process from house to house ringing the bells to protect the inhabitants and their flocks from evil spirits.

A great many folklore traditions surround the figure of the Green Man, who embodies the vegetative energy of nature. He is the ancient legendary guardian of woodlands, forests and trees, who keeps out of his territory any threatening ogres or other evil spirits. Images of the Green Man, with his head emerging from foliage, have been found all over the world, but he is most closely associated with northern Europe. In England he is personified as "Jack-in-the-Green", a leaf-draped character associated with traditional May Day revels, such as the chimney sweeps' festival still held in Rochester, Kent. His prancing about was held to ward off evil from every house he passed, and from the township in general.

In Scotland and northern England, the old Norse custom of "first-footing" is still observed. A dark-haired man must be the first person to step across the threshold of a house immediately after midnight on the last day of the year. This is to bring luck to the household during the year ahead – in

△ Wood from the birch tree was traditionally used in cleansing rituals, to expel evil spirits and to drive out the spirits of the old year.

▽ The green, or "wild", men of Europe signified the uncontrollable energy of nature, and their dances were often part of feasts and festivals.

through the gap between them in order to cleanse them of the influence of any evil spirits. (As a bonus, the process also got rid of cattle ticks.) The villagers would then throw a party and jump over the bonfires themselves to benefit from the magical cleansing process and bring good luck. The tradition of "leaping the Beltane fires" has never entirely died out, and is still enacted by Wiccans and other pagans.

Throughout the world, the warmth and atmosphere of a friendly fire has always been recognized as a "magical aura" of safety and protection from the powers of darkness. This may be why chimney sweeps and unglamorous lumps of coal have inherited their reputation as bringers of good luck.

A need to feel that some kind of spiritual energy safeguards the places we enter has always been present in the background of our society. Even though most people are unaware of the origins of the traditions they observe or participate in, the old customs thrive because they are still relevant to our spiritual life in the modern age.

▽ Many pagan festivals were associated with light, as the bringer of life, and candles and other flames are still used in modern ritual.

△ The warmth of an open fire in winter conjures light, life and comfort from the cold. It is also a link with the fire festivals of the past.

other words, to clear its space of "negative energies". Very often, the first-footer brings with him a lump of coal, intended as a magical token to ensure that there will always be the warmth of a friendly fire in the home. The first-footer may also bring some bread and some salt, symbolizing a plentiful supply of food. He must not carry any weapons or sharp tools, and no one in the house must speak until the coal has been placed by the fire and the first-footer has poured a glass of whisky and toasted the head of the household.

clearing personal space

Another New Year folk tradition is wassailing, the giving of a salutation for good health and wellbeing with a cup of spiced ale, to clear away any evil spirits residing within a person's body. The term "wassail" comes from the Anglo-Saxon *wæs hæl*, meaning "be whole" or "be well". There is a story of this traditional personal space clearing toast being offered to Vortigern, last Roman king of Britain, in the sixth century.

The night of 30 April to 1 May constitutes the pagan festival of Beltane. This is a fire festival whose name is Gaelic for "blaze-kindling". It used to be the custom for the pagan priesthood to light two fires, and for the villagers' cattle to be driven

Wisdom for the modern age

The principles of keeping spaces clear remain the same today as they have always been. Where once the services of the witch doctor or tribal shaman were employed, it is now the feng shui consultant, the dowser, the earth healer or the psychic who is most often consulted. Some of the most modern and sophisticated companies employ the services of space clearing professionals to alleviate or avoid problems in the workplace.

The feng shui practitioner might, for example, advise on a more auspicious placement of the furniture, or place a *pa kua* mirror in a strategic position to deflect negativity. The services of the modern dowser may reveal underground water-courses, electrical interference or areas of geopathic stress, and the dowser may suggest ways to divert the obtrusive energy around the building.

The psychic may point to restless energy fields or other psychic interference affecting the environment, and offer protective solutions. Experiments in the USA and other parts of the world to clear environmental pollution using earth acupuncture and assistance from elemental spirits have proved to be very successful. It may be tempting to scoff at unseen forces, but if such methods work, why not use them? Today, earth healers worldwide acknowledge and work with energy lines, just as Australian aborigines and other tribal cultures have done for thousands of years.

When considering why a space needs clearing, it is relevant to take into account unseen factors that can be the root cause of any problems the occupants are experiencing, such as geopathic stress or sick building syndrome, especially if the symptoms persist. The detection and correction of both conditions is best achieved by a professional dowser or architectural expert.

symptoms of geopathic stress

Geopathic stress is caused by disruption of the natural energy lines of the earth's grid system. These lines can be disturbed by any human activity, such as erecting buildings, damming rivers, or lowering water tables. Areas affected by geopathic stress can induce

◁ Traditional ways of using the land, such as these rice terraces carved from the hillsides, work in harmony with natural forces.

▽ When a modern metropolis is built without regard for the natural environment, it becomes a breeding ground for pollution and stress.

▷ Hectic lives in busy cities leave little time for the calm and quiet repose that is needed for health and wellbeing.

fatigue, depression, immune disorders, headaches, irritability, behavioural problems and insomnia. An environment affected by geopathic stress will affect all its occupants but not necessarily all in the same way. A general malaise hangs over the area, and its presence is often uncomfortably endured. These days dowsers are regularly called in to divert geopathic stress by using copper rods. Copper is a good conductor of energy, and by placing rods vertically in the earth the dowser can re-route the disturbed energy around an affected property.

sick building syndrome

This is another form of stress experienced in modern society. Its specific causes remain unconfirmed, but contributory factors seem to include external pollutants such as car fumes entering a poorly ventilated area, chemicals from indoor appliances and furniture, such as the fireproofing on upholstery and carpets, chemicals from office equipment such as photocopiers, and modern cleaning agents, as well as biological contamination from bacteria and moulds. Generally, lack of clean air, poor ventilation and the aggravating qualities of several chemical compounds together can lead to headaches, dry coughs, itchy skin, dizziness, poor concentration and fatigue.

The architecture of previous ages considered its surroundings and took a pride in its shape and form; our ancestors lived in homes made completely of natural materials. Modern building materials are treated with a cocktail of chemicals. Homes and workplaces are filled with fire-retardant chemicals, wall-insulation chemicals and cleaning fumes, and we also have to contend with external factors from the surrounding environment, such as emissions from factories, garages and agricultural farmland. Treatment for sick building syndrome is simple – it involves providing adequate, clean ventilation and removing the irritant factors as far as possible.

the modern world

In the past, our primary concerns would have been for the success of the crops, the welfare of our herds and our personal health and security. Today, in the developed world, our basic needs are largely catered for by the structures of society, so that our concerns now mainly focus upon success and achievement, prosperity and happiness. We live in a fast-paced consumer society, where more and more gadgets are provided for our use and entertainment, but it becomes increasingly difficult to find peace and quiet.

A century ago, most people were living far closer to nature. Even for those who lived in cities, travel was at a slower pace, often that of the horse or the bicycle, and everyone's day-to-day existence involved much more physical exercise and fresh air. Though life was undoubtedly more strenuous in many ways, many of the stresses we have to contend with in today's world were unknown.

As we fill our homes and workplaces with more and more modern technology, it is important that we do not become enslaved by it. We need to remain aware of the many different ways in which it can adversely affect the environment in which we live or work.

▽ Modern technology means that we can now travel the world with ease, but it also means increased noise and loss of green places.

Harmonious Living

It is difficult to reach a state of inner peace if our material surroundings are in turmoil, filled with clutter and riotous colour. Conversely, if we try to achieve a feeling of harmony in our physical environment, we find it easier to relax and unwind. In our inner being there is often another kind of clutter – mental and spiritual. If we can learn to encourage harmony in our daily lives, we will have taken a big inner step away from the oppressive weight of riotous environments, which scream for attention and produce spiritual negativity.

Outside influences

When we consider space clearing, we need to stop for a moment and think exactly what we are clearing space for. What is the actual purpose of this procedure?

The prime reason for space clearing is to enable us to lead a calmer life that is not oppressed by negative influences from our surroundings. In some rare cases this oppression may be attributed to astral entities – so-called evil spirits or negative vibrations – but generally it is emotional and mental static that requires clearing.

electromagnetic waves

One type of negative influence arises from the many technological advances our society has placed at our disposal, in the form of computers, mobile phones, microwaves, televisions and other equipment. Emissions from all these things can affect us and our surroundings. And powering all these items

△ There is currently a lot of research into the effects of living near high voltage electricity cables, which are suspected of causing ill health.

is another potential pollutant – electricity. The human body is electrodynamic, its functions regulated by electrical impulses from the brain. It stands to reason that electromagnetic waves from electrical equipment have the potential to disrupt or confuse our own electromagnetic field.

Nicola Tesla (1856–1943), the Serbian-American inventor of the alternating current generator, conducted experiments to show that electromagnetic waves do indeed have an effect on biological cells. In the 1930s, Royal R. Rife invented a variable frequency radio transmitter that produced mechanical resonance in the cells of organisms. The vibrations were capable of destroying the cells, and it appeared that the device could be used to eliminate cancer cells. On the other hand, some types of cancers and leukemia are thought to be caused by the presence in the body of free radicals, highly volatile cells produced in response to various environmental triggers, including manmade electromagnetic fields. Such findings indicate that electromagnetic waves can and do affect

their surroundings, and this should be carefully considered when you are using equipment that emits them, or deciding on its position in a room.

Regular, prolonged use of electronic equipment can result in a range of physical symptoms. Unlimited use of high frequency equipment such as mobile phones may lead to headaches, nausea, behavioural changes and immune system stress. The symptoms caused by low emissions (from computers, for example) can include lowered appetite,

▽ People living or working beneath the flight paths of major airlines are subjected to the stress of regular bursts of disruptive noise.

▷ If your work involves the use of a computer, you should avoid sitting in front of it for too long, and take regular breaks.

◁ Mobile phones and other electrical appliances emit electromagnetic waves which can have subtle effects upon our energy, leading to increased stress levels.

number of blends have been specifically formulated to deal with electromagnetic or radiation problems. However, the best defence is to keep your home and workplace earth-frequency friendly – that is, as natural as possible.

If the result of performing a space clearing exercise serves only to give you more time and inclination to split yourself away from true and basic human values, then no good purpose has been served at all. But if you follow a space clearing ceremony with time in the company of your family or friends, sitting together in the room without the distractions of television, video or computers, valuing each other's company and enjoying a fulfilling conversation, the newly cleared space will be charged with vibrations of warmth, love and companionship.

▽ Time spent absorbing the energies of the natural environment, is an effective antidote to the adverse influences of modern technology.

low blood sugar levels, nervous disorders, increased adrenaline production, and the build-up of static in the body.

Apart from the dangers of emissions, some other potential pitfalls need to be set against the advantages we derive from modern technology. We need to be aware of technology's effect on the time we spend with those we care about. For instance, people can easily make their living space feel hostile or tense – making any prior space clearing activities rather pointless – by arguing about what to watch on television. Microwave ovens have speeded up food preparation, but they have also meant that fewer people get together regularly to share meals with their family and friends. For some, the computer becomes an electronic "friend", isolating them from real life.

The challenge that these convenient devices present to our human values and behaviour patterns should not be underestimated. It has been said that there is no such thing as "black" magic, only magic used for bad purposes. This distinction applies equally to science and its innovations. Every technological device can be used for both good and harm.

coping with technology

You can lessen the physical effects of electromagnetic emissions by using technology sensibly. For instance, you can limit your use of a mobile phone, and take regular breaks from looking at a computer or television screen. Sit at least 3m (10ft) away from the television. Emissions can also be controlled to some degree by switching equipment off when it is not in use, rather than leaving it on stand-by. Earth yourself regularly by walking barefoot outside, and generally spend as much time as possible outside in a natural environment.

As natural parts of the earth's structure, the energies of crystals are radiated at natural frequencies, and you can use these to help balance the emissions of modern appliances by placing amethyst crystals around equipment such as televisions and computers. To remain effective, the crystals will need to be cleansed once a month at the full moon. To do this, submerge them in salted spring water and leave them for eight hours before rinsing them, or place them under running spring water or out in the moonlight overnight. As an alternative to using crystals, vibrational essences (such as Bach flower essences) can help, and a

The location of space

Where is space? The initial answer might be: "Space is all around us – everywhere." This, though, is not really true. The space that surrounds us is normally full of bits and pieces. Actually we tend to dislike space, although we may never have stopped to think about it. If there is a big space on a wall, we are likely to hang a picture there. If there is a large empty floor space, we put a rug on it. If there is an empty shelf available, we stand ornaments or books on it. An empty patch of garden can have a shrub planted in it. Most human beings are compulsive fillers of space.

The state of mind that produces this reflex action to "put something there" has been brought about by the steady increase in materialistic consumerism. We have become indoctrinated into the belief that success – and therefore "good" – equals possessions; that the greatest success equals the greatest number of possessions; and that failure – and therefore "bad" – equals lack of possessions. This is a thought-pattern that has spread throughout the developed world.

△ Uncluttered rooms decorated with simple themes of shape and colour can offer the senses both space and clarity.

finding space

Eastern thought has supplied the opposite philosophy: success lies not in possessions or material wealth but in freedom from their grip. This is an idea diametrically opposed to the driving force of a capitalist consumer society. The philosophy of Zen Buddhism is reductionism, which has a weak echo in Western society in the saying (more usually applied to fashion) "Less is more".

As an example of the difference between these two philosophical outlooks, compare a well-stocked flower garden with a Zen garden. Your own familiar garden may be filled with plants, a lawn, paths, seats, ornaments and a patio. A Zen garden, on the other hand, might consist of nothing more than a layer of gravel or beach shingle, with a single large boulder standing in the middle. Rather than filling the area with many objects and colours; the Zen idea is to draw attention to a defined space by virtue of the simple surfaces and textures contained within it. The beautiful flower garden encourages us to focus upon its contents: in contrast, in a Zen garden we are encouraged to become aware of the location of space.

▽ The sensitive placement of objects in a room can create areas or oases of calm in which to relax and unwind.

LOOKING AT SPACE

This mental exercise helps to train the mind to become aware of space rather than the objects that fill it.

When you look in any direction, try to make yourself aware of the spaces between objects, rather than the objects themselves, as though what you were seeing was a picture on paper and you were able to use scissors to cut out the objects themselves, leaving only the spaces between them. This exercise can expand the perceptions and help you to escape from preoccupations with the material world.

△ **The simplicity of the Zen garden leads the mind to concentrate on the space that is defined by it, rather than an accumulation of objects.**

This is not just a design concept. Coming to terms with it involves a fundamental alteration, even a reversal, of an entrenched point of view. By developing our awareness of the importance of space, we can actually nurture and improve the space in our own homes, rather than trying to fill it with displays of possessions and material trophies. By so doing, we can actually become aware of the location of space, and begin to appreciate the space that really surrounds us and in which we live.

Gaining such an awareness of the location of space is an important step in learning how to evaluate its character, and

◁ **A garden may be well cared-for and full of beautiful flowers, yet too cluttered and busy to inspire us with a sense of tranquillity.**

in sensing the ebbing and flowing tensions of the subtle webs of energy that course through it. If we can extend our awareness, our subtle psychic "feelers", into the spatial areas we inhabit and move within, we will be much better equipped to deal decisively and positively with any negative or oppressive vibrations (energies) we may find attempting to encroach upon us and undermine our emotional balance.

An awareness of space can help us to bring ourselves out of the habit of valuing possessions too highly. Preoccupation with the ownership of objects sets us at the centre of a cluttered world which limits us spiritually. To leave those limitations behind, we need to learn to value the release of such ties and anchors. In general, we too easily come to value objects for their own sake and not for what they represent. Once we can achieve freedom from the domination of material possessions, we can begin to set our spirit soaring.

The influence of colour

In any environment, colour can have a significant effect on the overall atmosphere. Hot colours will raise the energy levels of people in a room, and cool colours will calm and soothe. Confusion with colours can lead to confusion within human energy patterns. When you spend time in such a space, it can lead you to ask "Do I relax here or do I move about?" Therefore, when you are considering the atmosphere you wish to create in an interior, the first step is to decide whether you want the area to be a stimulating or a relaxing space.

Colours at the red/yellow end of the visible spectrum are stimulating, and colours at the blue/green end are soothing and relaxing. It becomes clear that to consider putting shades of red and yellow into a hyperactive child's bedroom would not have a calming effect upon his or her psyche. Conversely, if you have a lazy child who hates to get up in the mornings, a bright and vibrant colour scheme could be a very good choice. The same applies to any living

△ Water features bring the sounds of nature into a room and have a soothing effect.

or working space. Before you choose a colour for a room you should consider the characters of the people using it and the purpose or focus of the room. For example, a room where a lot of intellectual work needs to be done – such as a study or office – would benefit from having a yellow colour scheme. The bathroom, where you would wish to relax and unwind, could be decorated with colours from the blue/green end of the spectrum.

▽ A vibrantly coloured room may inspire you with the energy and confidence to face the day.

COLOUR EFFECTS
Within the broad division of the spectrum, each colour evokes specific responses.

STIMULATING COLOURS
Red: evokes confidence, power, strength and purpose.
Orange: invites brightness and joy, creativity and a positive attitude.
Sunshine yellow: encourages mental activity, stimulates thought, invigorates the nervous system.
Pink: as a blend of red and white, it holds the passions of red in check, encourages friendship, harmony in relationships and warm feelings.

SOOTHING COLOURS
All shades of blue: cooling and calming to the spirit and to over-emotional people, but can be unfeeling and cold if over-used.
Violet and mauve: warmer than blue because they contain a certain amount of red, these colours blend activity with rest and work well in living and dining areas.
Green: as the colour of nature, green is the harmonizer of the heart, helping us to be ourselves and to feel at peace with our surroundings.
Pastel colours: gentle on the eye and perfect for balancing any bright and colourful decorative objects.

◁ A blue interior can be very calming and soothing to the spirit. Splashes of orange and red prevent the overall effect becoming too cool.

colour and Ayurveda

Ayurveda is the ancient Indian science of life. It acknowledges three basic personality types, or *doshas*: fiery, airy, and watery. Everyone is a mixture of the three types, but in most people one quality is dominant. If the dominant dosha becomes too strong it can lead to problems, so it needs to be brought back into balance.

In Ayurvedic terms a fiery personality (*pitta*) is a blend of water and fire. This active, creative and sometimes dominant personality benefits from the blue/green end of the spectrum. Someone of this type finds it hard to relax. Therefore indoor fountains, plant displays, natural furniture and an appropriate blue/green colour on the walls will help to calm and balance the fire. With too much stimulation, this personality will be unable to unwind and relax. A fiery personality who occupies a red room is likely to become a bad-tempered workaholic.

The airy personality (*vata*) benefits most from surroundings decorated in warm and earthy colours such as terracotta, sand yellow, creams and warm browns. These colours help to earth this particular personality type, which has a tendency to drift off and perhaps not achieve everything it sets out to do. Full of ideas, the airy personality often has several projects on the go at the same time, never quite getting the time to finish them off. The airy personality benefits from an environment that features rocks and stone, natural earthy fabrics such as canvas and cotton, and objects that evoke safety and warmth, such as rugs and cushions, with gentle, subdued lighting. This personality would find it hard to live with the brighter yellows.

The watery personality (*kapha*) is a blend of water and earth. These people are emotional by nature, very sensitive but with a tendency to be inactive or insecure. Ideal colours for the watery personality type include pink, mauve, red, yellow or orange. Moving water helps to encourage their activity and dynamism in expression. They would not be suited to cold blues.

colour and the elements

Each of the four traditional elements – Air, Fire, Water and Earth – has a colour associated with it that is balanced by a complementary colour. Air is represented by yellow, which is balanced by violet. Fire is represented by red, which is balanced by green. Water is represented by blue and balanced by orange, and Earth is represented by shades of green, balanced by shades of red. From this it becomes clear that a room can contain a complementary clash of colours that will still have the same ideological focus. For example, a fiery room can include orange and blue and still be a room that conjures activity and creativity.

When we want to use colour to good effect, a little research can go a long, long way to creating the desired balance at home or at work, so that our surroundings don't clash with who we are.

▽ Take time to consider what results you are trying to achieve in your rooms and spaces.

A balanced interior

Human beings are governed and motivated in all things by their own psychology – the inner workings of the mind, particularly the unconscious mind. Since each person's mind is unique and has been formed by different events, thoughts, experiences and genetic sequences, no two people have identical feelings, tastes or preferences. Therefore the ideal surroundings for one person may be considered jarring, tasteless, or lacking in harmony by another.

It is impossible to say that there is a single correct standard for everyone to adopt in order to ensure that a room, or their whole home, will be perfectly balanced for all those who live in it or visit it. There are, however, some general ideas and suggestions that individuals can adapt and adjust with intelligence and perception to suit their own unique needs.

These obvious but simple measures can affect us deeply at an unconscious level. When we spend time in rooms that have personal meaning, awareness of space and ease of access, we experience uplifted spirits, contentment, relaxation and the enhancement of inner tranquillity and peace. If we plan our interiors with sensitivity and care, we can create the states of mind we desire by the way we orient and theme our home or workspace.

placement and movement

Some guidelines for the planning process are fairly obvious and universal. For example, it is important not to have a lot of clutter or items of furniture placed too near the access points of a room. When you are planning the layout of any room, you need to concentrate on the room's function and how people are going to use the space. In the case of a bedroom or an office, this may be a fairly simple task, but your living rooms may need to fulfil a range of functions, with members of the family pursuing different activities in the same space.

You can enjoy finding the best-looking placements for decorations and furniture, but you should not lose sight of the use to be made of them and the access that will be

△ **The careful placement of a few sensitively arranged items can provide a stunning focal point in a room.**

◁ **Choose furniture that fits harmoniously into its surroundings; a symmetrical arrangement can create a satisfying visual balance.**

needed. For example, a bookcase may look lovely beside the door, but it will not be such a good position if someone entering the room in a hurry throws the door open against a person who is looking for a book. Allow for the opening of cupboard doors and drawers, and don't place other pieces of furniture so close to them that they are difficult to use.

You should also visualize all the "roads" in a room. Every room has routes within it that are frequently used. At its simplest, this may be the route between the sofa and the television, or between the dining table and the kitchen. Plan around these routes, keeping them clear of anything that may impede direct progress.

▷ The routes people take when moving around your home should be kept clear and unobstructed by furniture. Easy access into and around the kitchen is especially important.

decorative themes

It can be effective to follow a particular theme in a room, or even within certain areas of a room. This is part of the art of successful interior design. Homes and offices are divided into specific areas precisely for this reason – offering a basic theme for each room, such as eating, relaxing or sleeping.

How rooms look should reflect their purpose. In general terms, the bedrooms should be calming and peaceful, the kitchen bright, warm and practical, the sitting room comfortable and relaxing. The use of colour is an obvious way to create a warm, welcoming atmosphere in a room, but other themes can be used to give a sense of unity to your decoration. A room might have an ethnic feel, for example, or be furnished with pieces from a particular period.

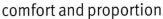

△ When placing decorative objects around the home, remain aware of thoroughfares so that you do not create obstructions and precious items remain safe.

comfort and proportion

Furniture should be in proportion to the size of the room so that it doesn't seem overcrowded. Even the most comfortable sofa will begin to look uninviting if it is at odds with the rest of the room. You also need to strike a comfortable midpoint between starkness and fussiness. In most cases, you will be furnishing rooms with items you already possess, but it is worth looking at all your furniture objectively to decide what you really want to keep and what would be better replaced.

Lighting can have a profound influence on the atmosphere of a space, creating excitement and drama or a sense of relaxation. Installing adaptable background and accent lighting means you can change the mood at the flick of a switch.

Avoid unnecessary and irritating clutter, and balance the contents of your rooms. By doing so the rooms' appearance is pleasing to the eye but also, equally importantly, to the soul, and you will be able to create harmonious interior spaces that generate feelings of spiritual comfort and inner wellbeing, whatever your personal style.

◁ To induce peaceful sleep, a bedroom needs to feel calm and balanced, uncluttered but also not too stark and minimalist.

Spatial harmony

The physical contents of an area are important contributors to our sense of peace and comfort, but the physical dimension works best when it forms the foundation for achieving the same conditions on a spiritual level. This is sometimes called the "spatial" level because it provides space for the energies that contribute to our wellbeing. A simple space clearing ritual can be used to promote spiritual tranquillity, and effectively to de-tox the spiritual atmosphere of the room. This can lead us to feel supported and nourished by our living or working space, rather than overwhelmed by its clutter, whether this is on a spiritual or physical level.

a ritual for harmony

This ritual is designed to bring home the fact that there is far more to the cosmic whole than is normally experienced. It enables you, spiritually, to step outside yourself into a greater moment, gaining a wider perspective of the universe and your place within it. From the centre of yourself, the warmth and comfort of this broadened vision of life will spread out into the environment of the area you are in, calming negative vibrations and bringing in their place a feeling of great peace and tranquillity, clearing the space around you of all disruptive energies.

Just after the sun has set, or during the early evening, lay out a simple altar with two white candles, a cup or bowl of water, a small heap of salt in a saucer or bowl, a small green houseplant, and some lotus incense in a holder.

Light the candles and incense. If possible, play some quiet, relaxing music in the background. Kneel calmly facing the altar. Relax your body, mind and emotions, allowing the mystical atmosphere you are creating to envelope your senses.

Lower your head with your eyes closed while you take a few slow, deep breaths. Repeat the following:

I see flame. Flame is energy. Energy is vibration. There was fire and energy at the beginning of all things. This fire and energy were caused by me. Thus do I confirm my identity with creation.

Take a pinch of the salt and gently sprinkle it into the cup of water, then sprinkle a few drops of water from your fingertips over the altar. Next, pick up the plant carefully in both hands and contemplate it. Become aware of its natural beauty, colours and shape, and say:

This plant is energy. It is the latest generation in an unbroken chain from the beginning of all life. Its ancestors caused it to be here and now. These flames I see were not, but I caused them to be here and now. Yet were flames ordained also at

△ **Before beginning the ritual for harmony, light the candles and some lotus incense, and spend some time in meditation.**

the beginning. Thus was this living plant ordained, and thus was I, too, ordained to be here with them now at the joining together of our lines through eternity. So with all energy. So with all life.

Replace the plant carefully on the altar, considering how profound the plant's life is. Then repeat the following:

I see the sun and I do not question it. I see the stars and I do not question them. I see the seasons and I do not question them. Sunset and sunrise, I question them not, but behold they are beautiful even if no eye sees them.

ATMOSPHERES OF A SPACE

When we spend time in an area, we react to its atmosphere on a number of different levels, both consciously and unconsciously. Broadly speaking, this can be divided into four categories.

Physical atmosphere: the material level, which is tangible and solid. It includes the structure of the space, the furniture in it and all the solid, visible items.

Emotional atmosphere: the feeling level. It influences mood or sentiment, creating feelings of peace, inspiration or creativity through the use of colour, texture and shape. It can be described as the comfort factor.

Mental atmosphere: the formulative level of ideas, thought patterns and judgement. The use of colour, shape, sound and light can raise or lower mental activity. A simple example would be the use of bright or subdued lighting.

Spiritual atmosphere: the spatial level. It influences our state of being and gives meaning and depth to the other atmospheres of an environment, providing the space for particular energies to exist. The spiritual atmosphere around us provides a meaningful connection between the seen and unseen worlds.

△ **Add a little salt to the bowl of water, then dip your fingertips into the water and sprinkle a few drops over the altar.**

This ends the ritual. Stay for a few moments in quiet contemplation, aware of your thoughts, feelings and the calming spiritual vibrations produced by the ritual.

△ **As you hold the plant in your hands, appreciate its unique beauty and sense its natural energy.**

▽ **Do not hurry through this ritual but spend some time during it to sit back and think about the words you are repeating, and sense the spiritual atmosphere you are creating.**

Pause for a few moments to contemplate your words, then finish the ritual with the following:

I have now seen myself, and I do not question it. I see myself in the light of a greater truth. I am a reflection in the eye of the universe. I am part of the Infinite throughout time from the first moment that ever was. [Here extend your arms towards the candles.] *May this light never be extinguished in my heart, but be with me through all times and all seasons. So shall it be.*

Inner space

As well as clearing the space around us, we need to learn ways to keep our inner environment clean and clear. In simple terms, we can view ourselves as having four layers: physical, emotional, mental and spiritual. In order to maintain a harmonious inner space, ideally we need to consider all four levels.

the inner you

Physically, your inner space will be influenced by your lifestyle and what you choose to eat and drink. You may like to consider changing things in your daily life that do not really serve you – or are actually harmful to you – such as too many late nights, poor eating habits, or addictive patterns such as alcohol or drug consumption. On a physical level, it is helpful to be more disciplined about transcending your "bad" habits. A weak physical level can significantly affect your emotional, mental and spiritual health.

On an emotional level, you should consider the effect your moods and emotions have on your environment. Again,

△ Inner space is as important as the space around us. Regular relaxing yoga routines are very helpful to the inner state.

self-discipline and working to understand your emotional make-up will help to alleviate heated arguments, stress levels and heavy atmospheres. At this level, you need to consider "relationship" – how you relate to the world and from what emotional perspective you see things. When you look closely at your emotional responses to life,

you may realize that they are out-dated, linked to wounds from the past that have yet to heal.

On a mental level, it is normally a cluttered mind that suffers mental stress, anxiety, insomnia or depression. Albert Einstein said: "A clever mind is one that is trained to forget the trivial." It is advisable to consider physical exercise, which is known to reduce stress levels, or to begin practising a spiritual discipline such as yoga, t'ai chi or meditation. The benefits of meditation have been well documented: it allows us to relate to who we truly are without falling into the common traps of everyday life.

It is what we are within, rather than what we do, that is the important factor. It is the soul or spirit of the individual that colours life and identifies his or her relationship with the greater whole.

◁ Drinking lots of spring water rather than coffee or tea will increase energy levels and reduce fatigue.

▷ Choose a chair for your meditation that allows you to sit comfortably but with your back straight. Place your feet flat on the floor and let your hands rest in your lap.

▽ Set an alarm clock or timer for the duration of your meditation so that you do not have to think about the time passing.

meditation for inner cleanliness

A period of meditation allows you the time and space to keep your inner world clean and clear, while at the same time creating space for spiritual harmony to filter down through the other layers. By spending time in quiet contemplation, you are creating an opportunity to simply be and so allow yourself the pause to catch up, or perhaps to unwind, without external stimulus or diversion. This enables you to centre and calm stressful states and thus bring about inner peace.

By meditating each day, you can subtly infuse your surroundings with balanced and peaceful vibrations, rather than the stress and anxiety of daily life. With regular meditation, you will feel revitalized physically, your mind will feel refreshed and your emotions calm. From here it is easier to step into each day with confidence and faith. Tasks become simpler to complete. It is as if meditation stretches time, and where before you may have felt the need to rush,

it is now possible to move at a pace free from stress and pressure.

Here is a simple daily meditation to keep you and your home, office or hotel room free from stress.

Set an alarm clock to ring after 10 minutes and place it beneath a cushion. Sit comfortably on a straight-backed chair with your feet flat on the floor, or sit cross-legged on the floor supported with pillows or cushions beneath you.

Imagine that your spine is being gently stretched upwards towards the heavens and at the same time downwards to the earth, and that the central point of balance is in your abdomen. Breathe fully, slowly and deeply, concentrating only upon your breathing. Breathe in "Peace", and allow the breath to infuse your whole being. Breathe out "Free from fear". At first your thoughts may race, your concentration may wander,

and you may feel restless. Simply continue to breathe and bring your mind back to the words on the rising and falling breaths. Gradually you will feel a calming influence as you maintain your focus on your breathing. Sit in contemplation until the alarm clock rings. On an outbreath, gently open your eyes and get up slowly.

▷ As you slowly open your eyes, imagine the sunrise coming out of your eyes and shining light on to a new day.

Outside space

The idea of space clearing seems at first to be connected primarily with indoor space. It is there that we understand how negative energy might influence us through our subliminal channels. We tend not to think that space clearing would be necessary outside – in gardens, parks, woodlands, or the natural world. We ourselves, though, are creatures of nature. It is because so much of our evolution as a species occurred in natural habitats that we contain the psychic biological networks that result in our ability to pick up feelings of ease or unease from our surrounding environment.

inherited instinct

According to fossil records, primates (the family to which humans, apes and monkeys belong) have existed since the Miocene period, approximately 25 million years ago. Our earliest known hominid ancestors,

▽ A day at the seaside, with its positively charged atmosphere, has a restorative effect that is both physical and spiritual.

Australopithecus afarensis, evolved over four million years ago, and our own species, *Homo sapiens sapiens*, appeared only within the last 50–70,000 years. This means that if we think of the entire existence of the primate family as being equivalent to one year, human beings have been on earth for one day at the most: and we have been "civilized" only for about an hour and a half. For all the rest of that vast span of time our ancestors lived on a hand-to-mouth basis with nature, in all her moods. It is small wonder, then, that we can still experience powerful instincts originating from our natural environment.

Our primitive ancestors possessed a useful survival instinct: when their "sixth sense" was disturbed it acted as a psychic alarm signal, making them extra cautious. We, in our civilized – or unnatural – world can still find ourselves feeling troubled, but we can no longer understand the reason for such a feeling: thus we believe we feel a "presence" in a certain place or at certain times. This is just as likely to happen outside as indoors.

△ As creatures of nature, we are just as sensitive to positive or negative energy in a natural setting as in our indoor environments.

▽ Salt is used ritually in many cultures. As a crystal it possesses the natural energy of the earth, and is a powerful cleanser.

△ The besom broom, which has been a traditional sweeping tools for centuries, is most commonly associated with witches.

space clearing outside

Any of the space clearing rituals described in this book will work outside in a garden or other open space just as well as they do inside. However, for many practical reasons you may not wish, or be able, to conduct a ritual outside. A simple solution is also the method for bringing the positive influence of nature inside your home: set up a nature table (also called a totem table) inside the room where the space clearing ritual for the outdoor area is to be performed. Even if no ritual is planned, bringing elements of the natural world indoors can help to unite our modern life with our deep instinctive responses to the vibrations of the natural world, enabling us to accept them and to feel easy in their presence.

To clear energies from the land, you can perform a "beating the bounds" ritual. This serves to chase away negative influences, and keeps your garden spiritually refreshed. Birch rods are used in the traditional ceremony of beating the bounds, but willow is also effective because it symbolizes purification.

you will need
> a birch broom or bundle of willow
>   twigs bound together
> natural rock salt

Moving in a clockwise direction around the perimeter, beat the ground with the broom or willow twigs, visualizing that you are chasing away intruders each time you beat. If you prefer, you can beat a drum rather than using a broom or a bundle of twigs. When you have walked all round the perimeter and returned to your starting position, walk round again, sprinkling salt very sparingly along the line you have just beaten, from start to finish, making certain that the end of the salt circle joins up with its beginning. (Remember that salt can harm plants, grass and soil: keep it to paths and sterile areas.)

▽ Tie a red ribbon on to trees or bushes, such as evergreens like ivy or thorn trees, outside your home to protect it,

A NATURE TABLE

Making a nature table is easy and enjoyable: it is simply an arrangement of natural items brought in from outdoors. For example, you can choose stones and small rocks, pieces of bark, mosses and lichens, twigs and small branches, acorns, roots, leaves, dried plants, flowers and feathers. The purpose of the exercise is to link the natural world with the modern environment and to remind you of your origins.

The Tools of Space Clearing

The most daunting of tasks can be successfully carried out with the right tools. They are important to human beings – for whom the twin foundations of knowledge and the use of tools have been the basis of success as a species – and like all skills, space clearing has its special implements. Whether you choose to follow a particular magical tradition such as Wicca, or take a more general approach, there are many things that can help to enhance your rituals and spiritual actions.

Scents and aromas

In the world of sensation, scents and fragrances play a very important part in controlling our feelings and responses. Smell stimulates a response by association, sometimes triggering clear and detailed memories of past experiences that we had long forgotten.

Foul or acrid fumes repel us, whereas sweet or fragrant aromas tend to draw us closer to their source. This is the basis for the choice of the different scents and incenses used during particular space clearing rituals. Just as they attract or repel us, some scents attract negative vibrations and others drive them away.

In the human world, our natural reaction to unpleasant smells is to try to get away from them, but in the spirit world, negative vibrations are attracted by dirt, dust, debris, carrion and uncleanliness, because they have the opportunity to "feed" off the presence of energy that is being held there. This is the reason why cleanliness is considered so important as a way to keep spaces clear of old or stale vibrations.

△ Scented flowers used as decoration in the home send subtle messages to the brain as well as stimulating the senses.

▽ The sweet scent of the jasmine plant can help to keep the atmosphere positively charged once a space has been cleared.

repelling negativity

In situations where a strongly negative atmosphere is experienced and serious space clearing is needed, the ideal aromas to drive away negativity are hot, spicy, vibrant and dynamic. These fiery scents include asafoetida, fumitory, pepper, garlic and chilli. Asafoetida, in particular, smells so foul when it is being burnt that the natural human response is particularly averse. This has the psychic effect on the person performing the space clearing of pushing all negativity away with a force of repulsion as strong as the smell itself.

The same principle applies to the use of fumitory – a herb used to expel negative vibrations of a lesser nature. The dried herb is sprinkled on to hot charcoal and fumigates the room with a smell that we would not consider particularly pleasant. However, it serves the purpose of clearing the room of psychic debris before it is filled with any positive input or charge. Both asafoetida and fumitory can be used to clean a space in situations where you need to

▽ Hot, spicy aromas such as garlic, pepper and chilli are associated with the fire element and are all strongly protective.

PSYCHIC ATMOSPHERES

You can perform a simple test using a lighted candle to see if the psychic atmosphere of an area is clear. All you need for this is a candle and holder, matches and an absence of draughts.

Fit the candle securely into its holder and stand it on a table that is out of any draughts. Light the candle and sit quietly and calmly by the table, but far enough away so that your breath does not disturb the flame. In a well-balanced room, the candle flame should burn gently with a small golden yellow flame, flickering only now and then, perhaps in the natural movement of air in the room. If the candle flame sputters, burns blue, behaves erratically, jumps rapidly or sparks, you have confirmation that the psychic atmosphere is charged and would benefit from a space clearing.

△ **Sprinkle some dried fumitory on burning charcoal to repel negative vibrations from a room, ready for a fresh beginning.**

"start again", perhaps when you are taking over a new office or moving into a new home. They can also be useful when gentler routines have not seemed to work for any length of time.

Once a psychically clean room has been established in this way, it is advisable to maintain the standard by making the space less attractive to negative energies – keeping clutter to a minimum, having a regular cleaning routine, and ensuring that life energy in the environment is positively charged by introducing healthy plants, dust-free carpets, fresh air, light and comfort. In this way, the space will serve you, rather than those things you are trying to avoid.

aromatic influences

Here is a quick guide to scents and aromas that will repel negativity, attract harmony and protection, or balance an environment. All the fragrances can be obtained in the form of aromatherapy oils, incense sticks, gums and resins or loose herbs. Use whichever form you prefer.

Aromatherapy oils should be added to water in an aromatherapy burner, gums and resins should be burned on hot charcoal in a charcoal burner, and loose herbs can also

be sprinkled over hot charcoal. The dried leaves of some herbs can simply be lit and left to smoulder in a suitable container, but you will need to experiment with the different herbs to discover which leaves ignite well on their own, and which benefit from the extra heat of charcoal.

Once a clearing has been established, a choice of balancing or harmonizing fragrances can be used to help maintain the clarity of the space and ensure a pleasant atmosphere for the occupants of the room. This acts to keep the space positively charged until it is felt that another clearing may be necessary.

These scents attract harmony and protection in any environment where they are burnt: frankincense, myrhh, lotus, rose and geranium.

These scents repel negative vibrations and can be used when a room needs clearing: cypress, juniper, fumitory, and sage.

These scents encourage and enhance feelings of peace and calm: bayberry, gardenia, magnolia, and rose.

Essences and remedies

Since the pioneering work of Dr Edward Bach in the 1930s, there has been a strong and steady increase in the use of vibrational remedies for a variety of physical, mental and emotional complaints. Bach developed a method of harnessing the natural energies of flowers by floating the blooms in pure water and leaving them for a certain time in sunlight, which draws the healing essence from the flower into the water.

From the humble beginnings of the 28 original Bach flower remedies, there are now thousands of essences from all around the world, covering a wide range of sources, from ocean to crystal, animal to tree. Each essence has its own particular qualities that are channelled into pure water and then preserved in alcohol. Vibrational essences act on the "subtle anatomy", or the body's life force, in a very similar way to homeopathic remedies. At this level, the essences work to influence and heal imbalances in energy patterns.

remedies to cleanse the body

Just as rooms and environments can be affected by undue negativity, so can the physical body. At times when stress seems overwhelming, emotions are running high, or perhaps deep fatigue from too many demands is hindering clarity and peace, any of the following remedies will be helpful in cleansing negativity.

△ Spritzing an area with water to which you have added a few drops of essential oils or flower essences can be a quick and easy way to lighten and clear an atmosphere.

White yarrow: works to strengthen the aura and acts as a shield against negative environmental influences.

Angelica: an all-round auric strengthener and protector, bringing the ability to cope with challenges or difficulties that could otherwise affect performance.

Crab apple: cleanses the body and soul of unnecessary or outdated vibrations.

Olive: an energy reviver that is helpful at times when you feel overworked, overwhelmed or just tired.

Vanilla: acts like a psychic shield, allowing you to maintain control of your environmental atmospheres without being affected by them.

Lotus: a spiritual harmonizer.

When you are making up a remedy mix, the order of application offers a map for the consciousness — an energy path for the psyche to follow. Adding the last essence encourages the energy to aim for spiritual harmony and peace.

A SPACE CLEARING ROOM SPRITZER

The following recipe can be made up and stored in a spray bottle. Spritz it around a room to clear negativity, emotional memories, mental stresses or psychic unrest.

The mixture is quick and simple to make and offers a convenient, quick-fix solution for clearing an atmosphere when time is short, such as cleansing between clients when you are at work, for example.

3 drops pine oil (purifies and refines energy)
3 drops rose geranium oil (atmospheric harmonizer)
3 drops cypress oil (closes astral doors)
5 drops lavender oil (mental cleanser and harmonizer)
7 drops myrrh oil (for consecration and protection)
7 drops crab apple flower essence (general cleanser)
1 tsp vodka
distilled water

Clean out a spritzer bottle with warm, salted water, rinse and allow to dry. Measure the aromatherapy oils and the flower essence into the bottle. Add the vodka, which preserves the mixture and allows the oils to blend more cohesively with the water. Top up the bottle with distilled water. Seal and shake gently to blend. Spray around yourself and your working or living area whenever you feel that the spirits need lifting or clearing.

▷ Honeysuckle flower essence is helpful when you are dwelling too much on past experiences and feel unable to move forward.

a cleansing mix

A mixture of the cleansing remedies can be taken when you feel you need an energetic protector and pick-me-up. Like all vibrational remedies, this mixture works by flooding out negative feelings. If you have been repressing your emotions, some unexpected feelings may be stirred up, but the remedy is safe and has no side effects.

Either place 7 drops of the mixture directly on your tongue, or mix 7 drops in spring water and sip it throughout the day. (If you are dropping it straight on to your tongue, don't allow the dropper actually to touch the tongue, to avoid the possibility of bacteria entering the remedy bottle.) While taking the mixture, avoid drinks containing caffeine, because it interferes with the remedy's healing path in the body.

you will need

> *spring water*
> *vodka*
> *7 drops crab apple flower essence*
> *7 drops olive flower essence*
> *7 drops white yarrow flower essence*
> *7 drops angelica flower essence*
> *7 drops vanilla flower essence*
> *1 drop lotus flower essence*

Rinse out an essence bottle with spring water. Fill the bottle one third full with vodka and then add the six flower essences in the order listed. Top up the mixture with spring water and shake gently to infuse the essences. Label the bottle "Cleansing Mix" and add the date it was made.

This essence can be kept for three months and should be stored in a cool, dark environment when not in use. If it becomes cloudy during this time, discard it and make up a fresh mix.

▷ To ensure inner balance, you can sip a cleansing mix of flower essences whenever you feel that stresses are rising in you.

Smoke and fire

Fire is intimately linked with light, and candlelight is often used during peace vigils and meditations to symbolize the spirit of remembrance and peace. Apart from its historical link as a symbol of light and hope, fire has also long been an instrument of purification. The ancient Celtic fire festivals, such as the winter festival of Yule, involved fires or beacons, not only to represent the light of life, but also to assist the community in driving away unwanted influences. A new log was kindled from the previous year's log, which had been extinguished, preserved and re-lit to ensure continuity and blessing from one year to the next.

In modern times, fire is used mainly as a source of warmth and not so much for its powers of cleansing and purifying, although there are several ways in which fire can be used in space clearing.

▽ The lighting of red candles in a room invokes the positive energy of Fire, the element of purification and transformation.

candles

The simplest way to represent the element of Fire in the home or office is with candles or lanterns, and one of the simplest fire rituals is to make an affirmation as you light a candle. This could be something like "May there be peace in this place", or "By the power of Fire, this room is filled with brightness and strength", or perhaps you might like to say "With this flame to protect me, no harm may enter here." The affirmation can be about anything or anyone you would like to call on to fill your environment. Your intent will be carried symbolically by the burning candle for as long as it remains alight.

When you are working with a black candle, light it and let it burn for up to one hour (but do not leave it unattended during this time) before extinguishing it and removing it from the room to be buried or discarded respectfully in the earth. You should then replace the black candle with a white one, allowing that to burn for

△ The symbolic act of burning away negativity serves to mirror that occurring in our lives.

REMOVING NEGATIVITY

A candle can be used to remove negativity by utilizing the flame to burn it away. This can be done by writing down those things you wish to release from the environment (such as the energy left in the room after a heated argument) and letting the written message be consumed by the candle flame. Once the paper has been lit, drop it into a fireproof container and let it burn to ashes completely. You can then scatter the ashes outside in the wind, as you visualize the negativity being blown away.

▷ Sprinkle some sacred herbs on to an open fire to conjure a mystical atmosphere.

another hour. As you light the white candle, affirm your call for peaceful vibrations to prevail in the place.

open fires

If you have an open fire, or a garden where a fire can be lit, you may like to build a stronger relationship with the purifying abilities of the Fire element by having that intention when you light the fire. Instead of simply laying a fire for warmth, add a handful of purifying herbs, with offerings to the Fire spirits such as a handful of peppercorns or a few sprinklings of tobacco. Add your intention that, as the fire burns, it will provide protection, and call for the spirits to be ever watchful to drive away negative influences from your home or land. The smoke from the burning herbs will infuse the environment with a protective haze. The open fire is no longer a place of winter practicality, but becomes a magical cauldron in which to gaze and observe the spirits as they dance away the dark.

▽ Laying flowers at the base of a candle can act as a focus for what you wish to call on or change.

colours, flowers and herbs

When you are working with Fire affirmations, certain candle colours will complement your particular requirements, and the following list offers a basic guide to colour correspondences.

To enhance an affirmation further, you can also surround the base of your candle with flowers or herbs chosen to complement and strengthen the focus of your ritual.

Red is for power, strength and protection, and is the colour of Fire; surround a red candle with carnations.

Black absorbs negativity and draws away psychic intrusion; surround a black candle with rue or sage leaves.

Green promotes harmony and emotional balance; surround the base of the candle with roses.

Light blue is for healing vibrations and peace; surround a blue candle with white jasmine flowers.

Pink represents love, romance, happiness and felicity; surround the base of a pink candle with pansies.

Yellow promotes change, new beginnings, wisdom and understanding; surround a yellow candle with lavender.

Orange is for healthy atmospheres, positivity and creativity; surround an orange candle with cloves.

White is for purity, balance and all general ritual work; surround the candle base with white lilies or camellias.

Music and sound

Sound is a form of vibration, which is at the root of our existence. Albert Einstein asserted that living things are not solid matter but a dance of atoms in space, and when we look closely at our physical nature, this is indeed the case. All matter vibrates, emitting waves of energy, and within a certain range of frequencies we respond to these vibrations as sound.

Sound can be used for protection, clearing or harmonizing, depending on the level and tone of the sounds used. Loud, shocking noises, such as fireworks or drums, for example, have long been used by many different cultures to drive out evil spirits. Conversely the gentle, almost inaudible, sound of a mother's heartbeat is capable of soothing a baby to sleep.

Our response to sound is largely determined by the associations we make with a particular noise. Sounds of nature can be stirring or soothing, as can music. For

▽ A gentle, repetitive sound such as a chime can be used to induce a feeling of peace in an environment that needs calming.

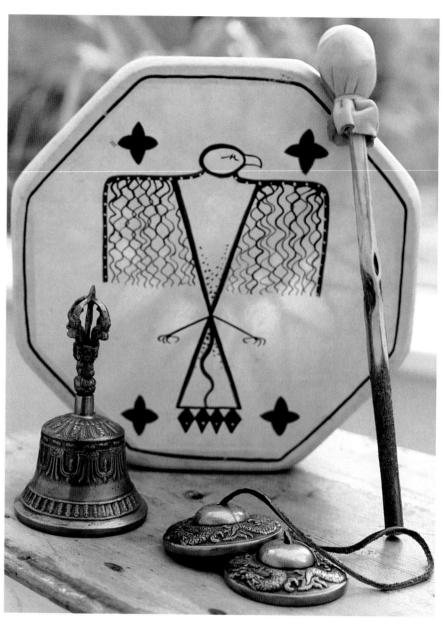

thousands of years the power of sound has been encapsulated in the use of voiced mantras and chants by many traditions throughout the world. Repetition of the "Aum" mantra, for example, can be used to harmonize an environment. It is a simple, safe and effective method. A variety of sacred mantras and chants can be sung or played, either to clear a space or to fill it with a particular vibration after a space clearing has been done.

△ Rhythmic sounds, especially in the form of drumming, are used in shamanic ritual to summon the assistance of the spirit world.

noise pollution

If you consider for a moment the myriad modern day sounds humans emit, which ride over and above the hum of earth's organic life, it is not surprising that noise pollution is now a well-established problem. Traffic, machinery, appliances, loud music

▷ Tibetan singing bowls can produce a variety of sound vibrations that touch the body with resonance.

and voices can all contribute to noise pollution. Many of us will have experienced a craving for peace and quiet as a result.

As we tune into the more subtle sounds of the earth, and simplify our lives, we have to acknowledge this orchestra of noise more seriously as a major contributor to stress and distress at home and work. We all need to consider how much we ourselves contribute to noise pollution, and take steps to naturalize and neutralize our part in it. By consciously filling our environment with more harmonious sounds and music, we can bring a depth and meaning to our world way beyond mere entertainment value. If you are looking for ways to naturalize the sounds around you, it is well worth exploring what is now produced by the New Age music industry. The sounds of nature and her creatures, such as whale song, waterfalls, or waves on the shore, are often found in the background of what is known as "ambient" music.

the powers of sound

Sound, music and the voice can all be used very effectively for space clearing. Fast or loud music and sounds will increase energy in an environment, whereas quiet, slow, rhythmic sounds will induce a sense of peace and tranquillity.

A drum, when played loudly and with authority, will help to expel negative energies, and when played rhythmically it will harmonize and raise the Earth element. Wind instruments, the didgeridoo, cymbals, tingshaws (Tibetan bells) and gongs can help to alleviate stress, mental chatter and frenzied atmospheres. Sacred instruments such as the bamboo flute, sitar or aeolian harp can also balance Air atmospheres. Crystal singing bowls can be utilized to balance the Water element, along with water features such as fountains, fish tanks and watery music. These are ideal for harmonizing emotions and for removing emotional conflict from living and working areas.

A MANTRA TO LORD SHIVA

The following mantra to the Hindu deity Shiva is a powerful way to clear an environment of any unnecessary vibrations, especially those that are blocking you personally, or stifling spiritual peace or understanding. Always burn a candle when performing this chant.

1 Sit in front of the candle and any representations you may have of Lord Shiva, such as a statue. Chant "Om namah Shivaya" (pronounced "Om narmar Shiv-eye-yah") rhythmically for at least 10 minutes.

2 If you have a set of rosary beads, you can perform the chant the traditional 108 times, moving one bead round with each repetition. For particularly difficult problems you can chant this mantra over a period of 40 days. The mantra can also be used as part of a regular spiritual practice, which will strengthen its influence upon you and your surroundings.

Crystals and pendulums

Because we are all subtly influenced by our environment and will be affected by it at a subconscious level, we may need help to reveal to our conscious minds what we are sensing subconsciously.

Crystals, as part of the earth's structure, emit energy waves at natural frequencies in harmony with our own biological make-up, and for this reason they can help to balance and harmonize our inner and outer environments. In fact, some parts of the human body are actually crystalline structures, including our teeth.

In dowsing, a pendulum acts in relation to our energetic impulses, revealing positive or negative responses to questioning, and we can use this technique to reveal the cause of a sense of disharmony.

▽ The amethyst is part of the quartz family of crystals and is safe and reliable for daily use in counteracting electromagnetic emissions.

using crystals

As children of the earth we need to acknowledge that we function best when we are in harmony with nature, and all kinds of crystals can play a significant part in maintaining that harmony.

Crystal clusters are excellent at keeping communal spaces clear. Their many points direct and charge energy positively, and placing a crystal cluster in a negatively charged room will clear it quite quickly. To clear negativity, use a smoky quartz cluster, to alleviate stress, use an amethyst cluster, and for harmonizing and emotional cleansing, a clear quartz cluster. If the problem is excess energy, crystals that will ground it effectively include smoky quartz, obsidian, hematite, chrysocolla, yellow fluorite, onyx and turquoise.

Modern electrical appliances give out electromagnetic energy at frequencies way beyond nature's own. To give an example,

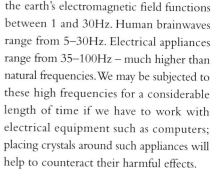

△ Many crystals, including turquoise, quartz and obsidian, have beneficial protective and harmonizing qualities.

the earth's electromagnetic field functions between 1 and 30Hz. Human brainwaves range from 5–30Hz. Electrical appliances range from 35–100Hz – much higher than natural frequencies. We may be subjected to these high frequencies for a considerable length of time if we have to work with electrical equipment such as computers; placing crystals around such appliances will help to counteract their harmful effects.

Rainbow crystals (those that have rainbow colours within them) placed on a sunny windowsill can work to bring the colours of joy to a depressed room. They also work well where moods need lightening. Rainbow colours are most commonly found in clear quartz crystals. Twin crystals are attached to each other but have two separate terminations at one end. They can be used to heal relationships and underlying relationship difficulties.

You can wear or carry any of the crystals suggested here by scaling down the size to smaller stones or single points.

⊲ **You can dowse using a pendulum to find out which areas of your home or office may be out of balance .**

indicate "yes" and "no"), to give it some kind of momentum to work with. To avoid concerns that you are influencing the outcome, after asking a question, empty your mind of everything except the words "I wonder what the answer will be?" and wait for the pendulum to respond.

To use a pendulum as an assessment tool for space clearing, draw a scaled-down floor plan of your chosen building, writing which room is which on your sketch. Hold a pendulum in your right hand. Place your left index finger on one area of the sketch and ask the pendulum "Is this room energetically balanced?" When you receive an answer, make a note of it. If the answer is "yes", move on to the next room. If it is "no", go on to ask a series of simple questions to discover what may be causing the problem, such as "Is this room emotionally charged?" or "Is this room affected by electrical emissions?" and so on until you find what is affecting the area.

HOLDING A PENDULUM
Hold the chain between the thumb, index and middle fingers, leaving about 15cm/6in above the pendulum free. Hold the chain with the fingers pointing downwards so the pendulum can swing freely.

dowsing
A simple dowsing technique can help you to discover if there are any areas of your home or workplace that are energetically unbalanced. Once any imbalances have been uncovered, you can correct them using whichever space clearing exercise seems most appropriate.

Before you begin, you need to discover which pendulum swing indicates a "yes" and which indicates a "no". The simplest way to find out is to ask a question such as "Is my name [*state your real name*]?" and wait to see what movement the pendulum makes. You will then know which swing means a "yes". To discover a "no" swing, ask the pendulum "Is my name [*state a false name*]?" and wait to see the movement.

Once you have established your "yes" and "no" swings, you can start asking questions. If at any time the pendulum behaves in a different way to your yes/no swings, it usually indicates that you need to re-phrase your question. A common error is to ask a question with more than one possible answer, such as "Is this room balanced or not?" It is important to ask questions of the pendulum that require a straight "yes" or "no" answer. If you reduce the question to "Is this room balanced?" the pendulum will be able to give a definitive answer.

Another common problem when working with a pendulum is complete lack of movement. To facilitate a response, dowsers may swing the pendulum to and fro (avoiding the particular movements that

Magical implements

Just about anything can be used as a magical implement, and throughout the history of magic, just about everything has been. However, over time certain tools have become paramount and in general they are associated with the four elements – Air, Fire, Water and Earth – together with a fifth, the Quintessence or Spirit, which unites the other four.

The magical symbol of the pentagram, the five-pointed interlocking star, represents this concept, bringing together the five elements that are necessary to sustain life: each of the four lower points of the figure represents one of the physical elements, while the topmost point represents Spirit. The pentagram is often traced during rituals and symbolizes protection and wholeness.

magic and the elements

Each of the physical elements has its own magical tool. The sword is associated with Air, the wand with Fire, the cup or chalice with Water and the pentacle with Earth. The athame (pronounced "ath-ay-me") is a general-purpose tool, which is used as a psychic pointer.

There has been some controversy amongst occultists regarding the correct tools to use to represent the elements of Air and Fire. Many magicians use the wand for Fire and the sword (or dagger) for Air, as

△ Shamans decorate their magical items with power objects such as feathers and claws.

▽ The traditional altar tools of the Wiccan practitioner are the chalice or cup, athame (knife), wand (stick) and pentacle (salver).

▷ The tools you use in magical ritual can be as simple as an ordinary black-handled kitchen knife and a glass bowl. The important thing is to use what feels right to you.

this is how they are depicted in packs of Tarot cards originating from the 19th-century occult Order of the Golden Dawn. Others believe that this was a blind intended to confuse the uninitiated and, instead, prefer to use the wand for Air and the sword or knife for Fire. But in magic, the only thing to avoid is worrying about it. The basic rule is to find the way that feels right for you and stick to it.

In the ancient past, magicians tended to be educated scholars and practised ceremonial "high magic". As they were high-born they were permitted to carry swords and therefore used them as implements for their magic. Witches, on the other hand, originated from the village wise-person. They were very often followers of the old pre-Christian fertility religion called Wicca and were usually advocates of "low magic". Witches did not have access to the ceremonial regalia of high magic and instead developed their tools from ordinary household objects such as bowls, platters and kitchen knives. They were usually well-versed in herbal lore.

The magical implement that is appropriate to any particular ritual depends on the nature of the ritual, or "working". Emotional matters are governed by the Water element, competitive matters by Fire, mental matters by Air and worldly matters such as finance and success by Earth. This is a very generalized picture, however. Another use of the Earth element, for instance, is in calming energies and dispelling hostile psychic vibrations, as well as for self-defence against occult attack. The idea behind this – as with electricity – is to run excess and unwanted energies to earth. Thus, the Earth element is regularly used in space clearing.

assembling the tools

A sword is probably the most difficult and expensive item to obtain, but like all the other implements can be purchased from occult suppliers. You can easily make the other magical implements yourself, using a little imagination.

The pentacle originated as a platter or salver. It can be made of any material, but is usually a round flat piece of metal or wood: a round wooden breadboard or coaster is very suitable, and you can paint a pentagram on it yourself. An ordinary black-handled kitchen knife can be used as an athame, and any glass bowl or stemmed glass from your kitchen can serve as a chalice. Much folklore is associated with the magic wand: according to tradition, it had to be cut in one slash on the last stroke of midnight. This is not really necessary, but it is a way of showing respect and gratitude for anything that you take from nature, and this is important.

▽ The Fire element can be quickly represented by a lit candle, and the act of lighting it takes on a symbolic meaning of its own.

THE HAND AS A MAGICAL IMPLEMENT

At times when it is not advisable or possible to use a blade in a ritual, you can substitute the fingers of your hand as a pointer, imagining that they are like the blade. The hand can be held in a symbolic position, in which the first finger represents Isis, the female, and the middle finger represents Osiris, the male. The thumb is positioned between these two fingers, and the posture thus invokes the protection of the god and goddess over their child, Horus.

Space Clearing Rituals

A ritual is an act repeated in a formalized manner to give it greater meaning and focus our concentration upon it, and ritualistic behaviour of various kinds helps to give structure and pattern to our lives. The application of rituals for space clearing greatly enhances our energy and determination, helping us to bring abstract knowledge into physical play to accomplish stronger results.

Preparing for ritual

One of the ways ritual magic works is through what is known as psychodrama, in which a physical enactment – involving sight, sound and the other senses – produces a corresponding change of consciousness, especially in the subconscious mind. This is the primal area of the mind – the basic and ancient root of the human consciousness. As the psychologist Karl Jung showed, it recognizes and communicates in symbols only, not in logical linguistics. Within it are stored not only our personal memories but also our racial memories, reaching back through thousands of years, which come up to the surface layers of our mind in the form of instinct. Some experts believe that we retain not just racial but species memories – that our deeper minds may contain the memories of our pre-human ancestors.

The subconscious reacts to enacted behaviour just as it reacts to real situations occurring spontaneously, so it can help if you treat a ritual like a theatrical production, learning your part as though it were in a play. Instead of standing self-consciously mumbling the words under your breath, this approach can encourage you to be bold with your movements and loud and confident in your declaration of the words.

purifying and cleansing the area

Any proper magical ritual, including space clearing, needs to be "written on a clean slate". If there are psychic impurities or negative energies present when the ritual is carried out, they can intrude and interfere, contaminating the result and sometimes changing it completely. As a modern analogy, we might think of such impure energy as a kind of "occult computer virus". A purifying and cleansing routine acts like an anti-virus programme. There are two areas that can benefit: the environment in which you intend to perform a space clearing, and yourself.

Every culture has its own favoured purifying and cleansing methods, from the Christian "bell, book and candle" to the pagan "rites of passage", and there are a great many to choose from. The simplest method is to burn a suitable incense and carry it round the area, calming your mind and projecting that calmness out into the room with the smoke wafting from the incense.

A slightly more intricate version, practised by occultists, is called the Rose Cross ritual. The lighted incense is carried around the room in a pattern, travelling from corner to corner, in a cross shape, then circling the middle of the cross. The shape resembles a cross with a rose in its centre, which is the symbol of the Rosicrucian Brotherhood, an occult order dating from before 1614.

▽ **It is important to approach an area you are preparing for space clearing in a dignified and respectful manner.**

▷ Keep a bowl of sand ready for when you want to extinguish the smudge stick.

smudging

The most popular purifying and cleansing technique is probably smudging, a shamanic method which has enjoyed a widespread revival in recent years. This method has several advantages. Its shamanic origin means it lends itself to just about any magical path without causing contention, so it can be used as a prologue to any kind of space clearing ritual. It is very simple but extremely effective and because it needs a little more input from you, it encourages magical thought and activity while you are putting together the basic tools for the ceremony: a smudge stick and a smudge fan.

The smudge stick is simply a bundle of dried herbs, usually including sage. The fan should be made of feathers, a single feather can also be used. The purpose of the fan is to waft the smoke all over the area, over the walls, floor and ceiling and round the doors, windows and any other openings into the room, such as the fireplace. The nature of the herbs and the intention of the person who gathered and tied them, together with the action of the fan, drives away any negative energies lingering in an area.

▽ As you fan the smoke, strengthen the action by visualizing the herbs' cleansing qualities.

MAKING A SMUDGE STICK

It is very rewarding to grow and dry your own herbs, thus ensuring that their magical qualities are tended during all stages of growth, and that you honour the spirits of the herbs when cutting them. The three herbs suggested here (three is a magical number) are all for purification. The best variety of sage to use is American white sage or mountain sage (*Salvia apiana*). All the herbs must be completely dry.

YOU WILL NEED

dried sage stalks
dried lavender flower stalks
dried thyme stalks
natural twine

Gather all the dried herb stalks together and arrange them in an intertwined bundle. Bind the stalks loosely with twine and trim the ends to neaten the bundle. Light one end, extinguish the flame, and let the smoke rise to fill the area.

Preparing yourself

For any ritual cleansing work, preparing yourself is a very important prerequisite. There is a saying that "cleanliness is next to godliness", and it is an esoteric belief that harmful negative energies – or evil influences – will fasten on to any dirt on the body of an individual commencing a ritual. (This applies equally to the clothing you are wearing, so fresh, clean clothes are also recommended.) Apart from this consideration, relaxing in a hot bath, especially one made fragrant with herbs, before a space clearing ritual serves to put the conscious and unconscious parts of the mind in closer touch with one another.

While you are bathing, imagine that you are cleansing away all impurities from your body and soul and, as the water runs out of the bath, visualize all those impurities draining away from you. You may like to anoint yourself with rose geranium essential oil diluted in some sweet almond oil.

△ Bathing ensures that all impurities are removed from the physical body prior to a space clearing ritual.

Alternatively, scent some almond oil with one or two leaves harvested from a *Pelargonium graveolens* plant you have bought to help with your magical and ritual preparations, thus ensuring a regular supply of the natural herb. Always harvest leaves with respect and care for your plant.

Another preparation often used, in religious activity as well as in magic, is fasting. This is a valid technique, as it helps to separate the mind from its material bonds by encouraging a semi-trancelike state. However, it is not an essential preparation for space clearing. You may like to consider a purifying diet instead, but check with your GP first as to whether this is advisable. If you feel that this is appropriate, you should begin the diet five days before you plan to carry out your ritual.

◁ You can anoint your body with rosewater or an oil blend containing rose geranium essential oil before performing a cleansing ritual.

▷ Preparation of your body and mind before you begin any ritual carries the same importance as the ritual itself.

mental and psychic preparation

It is important to be in the right frame of mind when undertaking any ritual work, so mental and psychic preparation is also recommended. For space clearing purposes, the correct frame of mind is relaxed, confident, at peace with yourself, calm, positive and assured.

After you have bathed, or made other physical preparations, a period of meditation immediately preceding the start of a ritual will help to achieve calm and composure. Space clearing is a spiritual process that can be quite draining, and its success will depend on your mental preparation and state of mind. Meditation can be accompanied by some quiet, spiritually inspiring music and burning a suitable incense, which should not be too thick or heavily scented: a light fragrance is best for the preparation before a ritual, leaving the heavier aromas for the ritual itself, in cases where they are considered to be necessary.

A banishing ritual can be performed after the meditation period. This will prepare the working area for the main ritual to come, and it will also put your mind into a receptive state for ritual work.

There are a great many things that can disturb the harmony of nearby energies: for example, a serious argument that took place the previous day between the couple living next door could have left "heaving" psychic vibrations, like a sea with a rough swell where there ought to be smooth water. Such vibrations can weaken the result of a space clearing ritual, or even make it completely ineffective.

A banishing ritual is like pouring oil on troubled waters, to smoothe psychic shockwaves. Such troubled vibrations can spread out over a surprisingly large distance, and they need to be eliminated before space clearing can be properly undertaken, so adequate preparation is an important part of the ritual itself.

HERBAL BATH MIX

All the ingredients for this mix are easily available to buy, or they can be grown in a herb garden or window-box. They are all associated with purification and cleansing. Use fresh herbs if possible.

Pile the herbs in the centre of the muslin square, then add the oats. Top with the rock or sea salt, pick up the corners of the muslin and tie with thread. Hang the sachet from the bath tap so that the water is infused with the essence of the mixture.

YOU WILL NEED

2 tsp organic oats
small square of cotton muslin
7 basil leaves
3 bay leaves
3 sprigs oregano
1 sprig tarragon
pinch of rock or sea salt
thread to secure

Banishing ritual of the pentagram

There is a particular ritual for general cleansing of the spiritual or astral environment that has been used by all the main magical disciplines for hundreds of years and is very highly respected. This is the Lesser Banishing Ritual of the Pentagram, which is called "lesser" only to distinguish it from its counterpart, the Greater Ritual of the Pentagram, used for magical invocation rather than for banishing (or clearing). This banishing ritual is divided

into three sections: the cabbalistic cross, the drawing of the pentagrams and the invocation of the archangels. Because the ritual is cabbalistic in origin, much of its wording is Hebrew (including a passage from the Lord's Prayer) and it uses Judaeo-Christian names for the energy forms that pagans refer to as Elemental Watchtowers or Guardians.

the cabbalistic cross

It should be noted that the hand makes the cross from right to left, not from left to right as in the Catholic crossing gesture.

1. Visualize a sphere of pure clear light, about the size of a football, a little way above your head. Reach up to it with the fingers of your right hand and strongly visualize that you are drawing a shaft of the light down to you by touching your forehead. Say the word "AHTE" (pronounced "Ach-tay" – "Thou art").

2. Touch your fingers to the centre of your chest, visualizing the shaft of light travelling down to infinity through the floor, as you say "MALKUTH" (pronounced "Mal-koott" – "the Kingdom").

3. Now touch your right shoulder and say "VE-GEBURAH" (pronounced "vay-Geboorah" – "and the Power"). Then touch the left shoulder, saying "VE-GEDULAH" (pronounced "vay-Gedoolah" – "and the Glory"). As you do this, visualize a shaft of light emanating from infinity to your right, crossing your body as you perform the action, and plunging away into infinity again on your left.

4. Now cross your wrists at the centre of your chest with the right wrist outermost, in the "Osiris risen" position. As you do this, say "LE OLAHM" (pronounced "lay-Ola-chiem" – "Forever"). Now bow your head and say "Amen" ("So be it").

the drawing of the pentagrams

The next part of the ritual consists of drawing four pentagrams in the air, one in each direction of the compass points, starting with the east. The particular pentagram used here is called the "earth banishing pentagram" (see diagram).

Each pentagram should measure from about shoulder to knee in height and should be drawn with the arm at full stretch if

▽ To make the first part of the cabbalistic cross, reach up with your right hand and visualize drawing a shaft of light down to your forehead.

▽ When you have completed the cabbalistic cross, cross your wrists over your chest in the traditional gesture of the god Osiris.

▽ Follow this diagram when you are tracing the pentagram. It is important to follow the direction of the arrows. Begin at point number one.

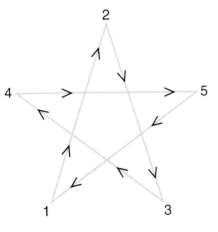

possible. As each one is completed, it should be "fixed" with a stabbing gesture of the fingers into the centre, accompanied by a key word in Hebrew.

1. Face the east to draw the first pentagram. When it is complete, fix it while saying the words "YOD-HE-VAU-HE". These are the names of the letters that spell the name of God: Yah-veh or, in English, Jehovah.

2. Turn to face the south and draw the next pentagram. Fix it with the word "ADONAI" ("Lord").

3. Then draw the western pentagram. The fixing word is "EHEIEH" (pronounced "Eeh-heh-yeh" – "I Am That I Am"). This is the name God called himself to Moses.

4. Finally, draw the northern pentagram. Fix it with "AGLA" ("Ah-geh-lah"). These are the initial letters of the phrase "Aith Gedol Leolam Adonai", "Thou art mighty forever, oh Lord."

the invocation of the archangels

The third part of the ritual is the invocation of the archangels.

1. Raise the palms of your hands to face forward and say, "Before me, Raphael!" ("Raff-eye-ell").

△ Having invoked the archangel Raphael with your palms facing forwards, turn them to face behind you for Gabriel.

2. Turn the palms to face behind you, saying, "Behind me, Gabriel!" ("Gab-rye-ell").

3. Lower the right hand, palm upwards, and say, "On my right hand, Michael!" ("Micch-eye-ell").

4. Lower the left hand the same way and say, "On my left hand, Auriel!" ("Or-eye-ell").

5. Then say, "For about me flame the pentagrams". Raise your hands above your head, put them together and say, "Above me shines the six-rayed star!"

the conclusion

To close the ritual, the first section – the cabbalistic cross – is repeated as before. Sometimes you might feel it is necessary to perform a banishing ritual after a main space clearing ritual, but usually just performing it at the beginning is enough.

▷ End the invocation of the archangels by affirming the power of the pentagrams.

Magical circles

Magic evolved through the ages into two broad types, referred to as "low magic" and "high magic". These terms are very generalized and the two often merge seamlessly together. Low magic was practised by the simple and poor: peasants who had no access to education, riches or reading and writing. This is the kind of magic that originated with the tribal shaman, or the wise woman mixing her herbs in a steaming cauldron. High magic grew out of it and became the province of the rich, the nobility and the educated.

As an example of the essential difference between high and low magic, a kitchen knife was often used as a "psychic pointer" in low magic, and this evolved into the athame, the ritual pointing knife used by witches. In contrast, the upper classes were permitted to carry swords, which were usually forbidden to the peasantry, and therefore in high magic a ritual sword is frequently used as a pointer instead of the athame. The magical implements used today no longer have any association of this kind with class structure. Today's witches use swords freely, and ritual magicians use herbs and athames.

◁ A handful of sacred herbs can be put into a heatproof container and burnt to raise bright vibrations in a room.

△ A visual magic circle can be created by forming a ring on the floor with night lights or small candles.

casting a circle

In both high and low magic, a magic circle is considered indispensable. The idea, greatly simplified, is that this creates what might be called a protective "energy field" around the place of working, through which no hostile or negative astral forces can penetrate. (Although it is seen with the eyes as a circle on the ground, the mind should perceive it as a sphere.) Casting a magic circle is an important part of witchcraft, or Wicca, which follows the traditions of the "low" magic of the ordinary people.

In casting a magic circle, great importance is attached to astral beings called the Guardians of the Watchtowers. The "watchtowers" are the four compass points and the four elements of Air, Fire, Water and Earth to which they are linked (Air corresponds with east, Fire with south, Water with west and Earth with north). The Guardians of the Watchtowers protect those who invoke their aid and ensure the security of the circle. In low magic, especially in Wicca, complex rituals and magical regalia are not normally used.

a simple space clearing

This can be used anywhere as a space clearing procedure, and is a short and simple ritual. But in spite of its simplicity, it is a powerful piece of low magic. As with any magical or mystical activity, you should prepare yourself beforehand. Make sure you

▽ Drawing a magic circle around yourself using an athame, or ceremonial knife, follows a tradition that is many centuries old.

choose a time when you will not be interrupted. A short period of meditation is recommended to calm the mind and spirit, and to eliminate all disruptive thoughts from daily life intruding on the ritual.

The first part of the spell involves casting a magic circle. For this, if you do not have an athame you can use an ordinary kitchen knife as a pointer, preferably one with either a black or a natural wood handle, or you can use your hand.

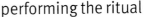
performing the ritual

Having meditated, stand facing north. Slowly raise the knife or your hand to point in that direction, then turn to the right to face east, imagining that you are drawing a line of pure light in the air as you move. Then turn again to face south, then west, then north again until the circle is complete. As you do this, repeat the following circle-opening invocation, saying each line as you face the appropriate point of the compass:

I call the Guardians of the North, protect this
*   place from earthly wrath.*
I call the Guardians of the East to calm the airs
*   and bring me peace.*
I call the Guardians of the South, protect me from
*   the fire's red mouth.*
I call the Guardians of the West to lay the stormy
*   seas to rest.*

When you have completed the circle, remain facing north, relax and say:

Let blessings be upon this place,
and let my Circle clear this space
of spirits wicked, cruel or fell,
so that I in peace may dwell.

Imagine the circle you have cast is spreading out through the universe like the ripples in a pool, bringing tranquillity and peace to its centre, which is you and your space.

▽ Ripples in water, moving outwards, will eventually be still and calm, like the space you have just cleared.

A zodiac ritual

This space clearing ritual draws on your astrological sign to personalize it and give it power. Use the chart of sun signs to select the correct corresponding tools and materials, and insert the name of your sign where appropriate in the wording.

All astral or psychic energies are intimately connected with zodiacal influences, but while virtually everyone has heard of the zodiac, fewer actually know its definition. While the earth makes its annual orbit of the sun, from earth we perceive this movement as if the sun is travelling along an imaginary line across the sky, called the ecliptic. The zodiac is the name given by astrologers to the band of 12 constellations that appear along the ecliptic through the year. During each 30-day period of the year, the sun appears to rise against the background of one of these groups of stars, and that constellation is said to be the sun sign of anyone born in that period.

The zodiac space clearing ritual has 12 variations which all use the same ritual framework, and there are two ways to choose the appropriate zodiac sign to include in it. You can either choose your own birth sign (or that of anyone you may be helping) or select whichever sign covers the date on which you are to perform the

ritual (you can check this in the horoscope section of a newspaper if you are unfamiliar with all the zodiac dates).

preparation

Set up the altar so that you will face east when standing in front of it. You will need an altar cloth, an incense burner, a small heap of salt in a container, and the four magical implements: wand, pentacle,

△ This variation of the zodiac ritual uses turquoise, benzoin and the chalice to fit with the sign Scorpio.

sword/athame and cup/chalice (all four should be present, even if only one is to be used in the ritual). Place the tool corresponding to the chosen zodiac sign near the front of the altar. The cup or chalice should contain a small amount of water, whether or not you will be using it.

the ritual

Light the incense and the candles. Pick up the cup or chalice and sprinkle a pinch of salt in the water, saying: "Thus do I cleanse and purify thee, oh spirit of Water, that thou mayest aid me." If you are not using the cup further, replace it on the altar.

Take up the appropriate magical tool and hold it out towards the east, at arm's length. State in a commanding voice:

By the ancient magic of [zodiac sign] *I call now upon the spirits of time and space to assist me in cleansing this place of all impurities. By this* [name of tool], *the symbol of the authority over*

SUN SIGNS AND CORRESPONDING TOOLS

SIGN	INCENSE	MAGICAL TOOL	CANDLE COLOUR
Aries	Dragon's blood, lily	Wand	Scarlet
Taurus	Storax, mallow	Pentacle	Red, orange
Gemini	Orchid, wormwood	Sword/athame	Orange
Cancer	Lotus	Cup/chalice	Amber
Leo	Sunflower, olibanum	Wand	Yellow
Virgo	Lily, sandalwood	Pentacle	Yellow-green
Libra	Aloe, galbanum	Sword/athame	Emerald green
Scorpio	Benzoin	Cup/chalice	Turquoise
Sagittarius	Lignum aloes	Wand	Blue
Capricorn	Hemp, musk	Pentacle	Indigo/black
Aquarius	Galbanum	Sword/athame	Violet
Pisces	Opium, ambergris	Cup/chalice	Crimson

again, repeating the action for the fourth and last time.

Replace the magical tool on the altar and cross your wrists over your breast, fists clenched, right wrist outermost (in what is called the "Osiris risen" position). In a very firm and commanding voice, say this:

Let no creature of any sphere now malign this place. Let all malignity depart hence, and all good enter herein. Let no disturbing influence or visitation descend upon this protected place.

Take up the cup once more, whether it was the main magical tool or not. In a dignified manner, carry it round the perimeter of the area you are clearing. As you go, sprinkle occasional drops of water with your fingertips. This forms a magical circle of protection around the area that hostile astral forces cannot penetrate.

End the ritual by returning to the altar, turning your back to it and announcing to the world: "Go ye in peace!"

▽ **When sprinkling your water in an area imagine it is holy water charged with light and blessings.**

△ **Be clear and authoritative when speaking the words of a zodiac ritual, believe in what you say.**

the occult powers of [zodiac sign], *I command that all that is hostile, of negative intent or malicious of form or mind, depart hence. Depart, I say, and return not, for the forces of* [zodiac sign] *stand now guard upon this place of enchantment. Thus is my will! Thus is my command! Thus is my power!*

Turn to the right so that you are facing south, thrust the magical tool forward in that direction and bark out loudly the word "AVAUNT!" (meaning "depart"). Turn to the right again to face west, again thrust the magical tool forward and say again, "AVAUNT!" Turn to the north and repeat the action, and finally return to face east

NATIVE AMERICAN SACRED HERBS

For thousands of years, the indigenous people of North America have maintained a very close relationship with the plant kingdom. They use many herbs for healing, protection and blessings, but their four most sacred herbs for purification and protection are sweetgrass, sage, cedar and tobacco.

Sweetgrass is traditionally used for self-blessing, for keeping evil spirits away from the home and to purify tools and equipment, because its sweet smell calls up the good spirits. It is plaited into a braid, then the end is lit and the smoke wafted over magical tools or around the room.

Sage is a powerful cleanser and purifier, and native Americans have been known to sit on sage leaves in sweat lodges, thus physically linking into its purifying abilities. The leaves can also be used for smudging, either loose or in smudge sticks. The most effective types are white or mountain sage and desert sage.

Cedar is an evergreen tree also known as the Tree of Life; it is a very powerful psychic and spiritual cleanser. Smudging with cedar is advised when conditions are particularly difficult or obstructive, as its powers deal with the more "problematic" energies. It can be obtained loose and dried, to be sprinkled on hot charcoal when required.

Tobacco is used for offerings to the Great Spirit and to the elemental and natural powers of creation. Tobacco is also cast into the sweat lodge fire as an offering to the fire spirits, and is sometimes given to elders and medicine men as a mark of respect.

The word "shaman" comes from the Tungusic dialect of the Ural-Altaic tribes of Siberia, but it is now used to describe individuals of many traditions throughout the world that commune with the natural and supernatural world.

The shaman employs sacred herbs, drums and chants to summon the assistance of the spirit world, in order to cleanse a person, situation or environment of any perceived negative or stale influences.

the ritual

The shamanic ritual outlined here calls upon the powers of the drum, of sacred herbs, and of the *inyan* (the stone people of the native Americans) to cleanse and purify an area.

YOU WILL NEED
loose dried sage
smudge bowl or shell
black or dark feather
large stone chosen for
*   its individuality*
tobacco
drum

▽ **Begin the ritual by smudging yourself and the large stone with smoke from the smouldering sage. Use a feather to fan the smoke.**

▷ Beat the drum while moving in a spiral around the room, towards the centre.

Place the sage in the smudge bowl and light it. Use the feather to fan the smoke around yourself and over the large stone.

Take a pinch of tobacco and stand in the centre of the area you are clearing. Facing north, say "Great Spirit, I honour you, and humbly seek your presence within this grandfather rock." Place the pinch of tobacco at the central point of the room. Pick up the large stone and, holding it to your heart, ask it to help you to clear the environment by absorbing any stray energies. Set the stone in the centre of the room on top of the tobacco, saying, "Mitake oyasin" ("For we are all related").

Take another pinch of tobacco and, still facing north, hold out your hand in that direction. Call with feeling and respect, "Buffalo." Place the tobacco on the floor to the north. Take another pinch of tobacco, face the east and call: "Hawk." Place the tobacco on the floor to the east. Repeat the gesture for the south, saying, "Coyote," and for the west, saying, "Bear."

Turn to face north again and now say, "Guardians of the four winds, I – your brother/sister – do call your presence here."

▽ Hold the grandfather rock to your heart and ask it to help you in your task.

Stand the smudge bowl on the stone so that the smoke coils up through the room.

Take up the drum and, beginning at the edge of the area, walk clockwise in a spiral until you reach the centre, drumming the atmosphere towards the stone. Drum over the stone into the herbs, visualizing the stray energies coiling away in the smoke. Thank the Great Spirit, grandfather rock, and the four guardians for their help. Repeat "Mitake oyasin" and remove the smudge bowl from the stone. Take the stone outside to rest on the earth in order to discharge any remaining energy into the ground.

▷ As the smoke coils through the room, sit for a moment and visualize the cleansing process.

A ritual in the Zen style

Zen is a philosophy of Chinese origin, adopted by the Japanese in the 12th century, that has its own unique identity within the wider practice of Buddhism. The name is derived from the Chinese word *ch'an* which, in turn, originates from the Sanskrit *dhyana*, meaning "meditation". The essential concept of Zen is that a true state of perfection – nirvana – is attained only when all is reduced (or expanded) to nothing. It cannot be reached while the surface of life ripples with emotion, desire, concern, ambition, curiosity or selfishness.

A number of "koans" (exercises in paradox) originate from Zen teachings and give an indication of what needs to be accomplished by the mind of the acolyte who seeks nirvana. Perhaps the most famous of these questions is "What is the sound of one hand clapping?" If everything is reduced (or elevated) to its ultimate state of non-being, perfection has been reached. Zen rituals, therefore, tend toward simplicity, quiet, stillness and deep inner reflection to

△ Zen epitomizes simplicity, and rituals in the Zen style are likewise always simple.

create an atmosphere of intense and almost solid peace; they are ideal for dispelling any form of psychic disharmony or negative energy in space clearing.

Because this ritual comes from the eastern rather than the western tradition, it is not necessary to precede it with a banishing ritual, though this can be done if you feel it is appropriate.

▽ **A room decorated and furnished in accordance with the philosophy of Zen will always reflect spaciousness and composure.**

PRONUNCIATION

"Aum" (or "Om") is spoken after taking as deep a breath as possible. It begins with the sound "Ahh", moving into "Om" (like the first syllable of "omelette") and continuing the "mm" for as long as the out-breath lasts. This word is held to symbolize all the sounds in the universe.

▷ **A clear mind is the perfected state of Zen. Meditation is an ideal practice to help you move towards such a state.**

preparation

Arrange for as much silence and stillness as the surroundings permit. If possible, use a gong to mark the beginning and end of the ritual: otherwise, find something else that will produce a similar clear, simple sound, such as a stone to bang gently on a small block of wood. You will also need a low table or altar covered with a plain black cloth and a few sticks of sandalwood incense in a suitable container.

Set up the altar as close as possible to the exact centre of the area you wish to include in the space clearing, so that you can sit or kneel before it facing east.

the ritual

Light the incense. Kneel on a cushion or sit on a straight-backed chair before the altar, or adopt the lotus position if you prefer. When you are settled, perform the fourfold breath to still your thoughts: to do this,

▽ **A simple sound, such as the striking of a gong or chime, is used to mark the beginning and ending of a Zen ritual**

breathe in to an unhurried count of four, hold your breath for a count of four, breathe out for a count of four and hold your breath again for a count of four, then take the next breath and repeat the sequence. Continue to practise the fourfold breath for a few minutes, until you feel a state of great calm begin to unfold.

When you feel sufficiently calm and at ease with your surroundings, gently sound the gong once. As the sound fades, begin to chant the single word "Aum" as slowly as possible. Keep your head bowed towards the altar. Repeat the chant 10–12 times, taking care throughout to avoid any feeling of "hurrying things along".

Once you have reached the end the chanting, take two or three more fourfold breaths, then slowly bow towards the east, with your hands held at your chest in an attitude of prayer. In this position, repeat a single long "Aum". Your mind should now be clear enough to concentrate your thoughts. Close your eyes and make your mental image as sharp as you can, aiming for a reality equivalent to having your eyes open. This may take a little practice before you undertake the ritual itself. Visualize a circular ripple of light in the centre of your abdomen, slowly spreading out horizontally, like the ripples from a stone tossed into a pool filmed in slow motion. As this circle of light reaches the horizon, it continues out into the universe and to infinity. Continue to observe this visualization for several minutes.

To end the ritual, stand up, place your hands in the prayer position at your chest as before and bow deeply from the waist. Sound the gong once more to close.

An angelic space clearing

The concept of angels is familiar in the Judaeo-Christian tradition, in which these high and pure spiritual entities act as messengers, protectors and guides to humans. Some, such as Gabriel, are mentioned in the Bible, and there are famous stories of angels being seen on battlefields or by individuals in danger, whose lives were saved by the angelic beings. Angels predate the Biblical period, originating in earlier cultures such as those of Sumer, Babylon and Ur (in modern Iraq). Angelic invocation formed the basis of many ancient occult practices, and individual angels were traditionally associated with various entities, such as the seven ancient planets, specific days of the week, certain colours, incenses, symbols and powers.

If you are attracted to this kind of spiritual conception, you may well draw the strongest benefit from performing an angelic

THE ATTRIBUTES OF ANGELS

Traditional correspondences exist for each angelic presence, and this list will help you to call upon the assistance of the most appropriate angel for your needs. In your ritual, utilize the appropriate symbols for the angel you choose.

ANGEL/CHARACTER	HELPFUL FOR	DAY	COLOUR	SYMBOL	INCENSE
Michael Angel of the sun, guardian and protector	Summon to encourage success, or with issues involving the maintenance of stamina or physical health	Sunday	orange/gold	six-pointed star	olibanum
Gabriel Angel of the moon, protector of women and children	Summon for fertility, healing, psychic abilities and all issues concerning harmony in the home	Monday	pale blue	nine-pointed star	myrrh, jasmine
Samael Angel of Mars, protector and guardian, guide to men	Summon to protect against violence, to dispel negative opposition and to obtain justice in your life	Tuesday	red	five-pointed star	tobacco, dragon's blood
Raphael Angel of Mercury	Summon to protect during times of change, upheaval or travel and for issues of mental stress.	Wednesday	yellow	eight-pointed star	galbanum, storax
Sachiel Angel of Jupiter	Summon when you are seeking justice, or protection of your financial situation or status	Thursday	purple	square	cedar
Anael Angel of Venus	Summon when conflict involves relatives or friends, where emotional harmony or love may be lacking	Friday	green	seven-pointed (or mystic) star	rose, red sandalwood
Cassiel Angel of Saturn	Summon in cases involving the protection of property, land or possessions, to clear obstacles suchas chronic health conditions, or in situations where you feel blocked by another's actions	Saturday	indigo or black	straight line	myrrh

△ Each angel has an association with a particular colour and fragrance: use the appropriate candles and incense on the altar.

▽ Light the incense and leave it to smoulder while you spend about 15 minutes each day in contemplation of your chosen angelic power.

▽ To end the ritual, extinguish the candles with respect and give thanks to the energies that will respond to your call.

space clearing. When an angelic presence is invited into the place you wish to be cleared, it will leave a lingering protective power and the strong influence of its own characteristics, which will make the place feel calm, tranquil and thoroughly cleared of all hostile or negative influences.

an angelic altar

When you have decided which angel is most appropriate for your needs, you can set up an altar to your chosen protector. This is done very simply by assembling two candles in the colour that corresponds to your angel, and the correct incense, perhaps with an image or symbol to focus your thoughts. Place a candle on each side of the incense container and write in appropriately coloured ink the name of the angel you wish to call upon, drawing the symbol of that angel above the name.

Light the candles and the incense and sit before the altar for about 15 minutes each day, asking for assistance and/or intervention on your behalf in dealing with the situation or energy you are trying to clear. Repeat your request three times and then sit quietly in contemplation of your angel and the help you will receive. Extinguish the candles with respect and give thanks to the energies that will respond to your call.

A druid space clearing

We know very little about the Druids of old, because they were members of a culture that kept no written records. The knowledge we have comes almost entirely from a few books written by the Romans, who were responsible for exterminating the Druids ruthlessly. The typical Druid seems to have been an athletic warrior who possessed remarkable knowledge. From childhood, he would have committed to memory the wisdom, culture and history of the Celts, all of which was transmitted orally.

The Druids were the priesthood of the Gaulish tribes, also known as the Celts, who populated west and central Europe in the pre-Roman era. Later invaders, such as the Anglo Saxons (who reached Britain from Germany after the Romans had abandoned the islands), pushed the Celts into the most remote areas of Europe, including Scotland, Cornwall, Wales, Brittany and the Basque region of northern Spain.

The Druids regarded oak trees and mistletoe as sacred: when we "kiss under the mistletoe" at Christmas, we are actually enacting part of an ancient pagan fertility rite. They also practised human sacrifice (often by burning their victims in groups inside wooden cages shaped like giant human figures), which was the Romans' declared reason for stamping them out. However, it is more likely that the Druids were destroyed because they were the intellectual leaders of Celtic society, and were capable of organizing resistance against Roman rule.

The modern order of Druids was invented in the 18th century, probably as a rival to Freemasonry, and has no direct

GOD OF THE EARTH
"Father Dis" was worshipped by the Druids as the god of the earth. The Romans equated Dis with their god Pluto and the Greek god Hades, the rulers of the underworld.

△ Druidic rituals were often performed in groves of oaks, the most venerated of trees and sacred in ancient times to the sky-gods.

▽ Today we are more often surrounded by buildings than the wonders of nature, but we can still express our respect for the natural world.

produce an aura of calm about yourself. When you feel calm, approach the east of the area. Stand and draw a deep breath. Without shouting, use the breath to declaim authoritatively: "There is peace!" Now approach the south, take another deep breath and again use it to declaim: "There is peace!" Repeat in exactly the same way to the west, and finally to the north.

Returning to face the east, adopt the occult salute of Dis, by crossing the forearms at the level of the forehead, with clenched fists. In this position, take another deep breath and state levelly and quietly: "I have peace! Let peace prevail!" Lower the arms and visualize the atmosphere of peace spreading like a white mist throughout the area. Gather up the twigs and burn them ceremonially outside or on an open fire indoors. If fire poses a problem, you can bury the twigs, preferably beneath an oak tree. In this case, let the oak tree know what you are burying and why.

△ **Having set twigs and boughs around the space to be cleared, arrange the candles and incense around the room and light them.**

connection with the Celtic priesthood. Some writers have suggested that Druidism and Wicca share a common origin in the remote past, and there seem to be some grounds for this. Wicca is known to be a combination of the native lunar-based agricultural tradition with the sun-worship brought by the migrating Beaker people of the Bronze Age, around 1500 BC. Thus Wicca observes four lunar festivals (known as the major Sabbats) and four solar festivals (the lesser Sabbats). It is possible that Druidism in Roman Gaul was descended from the sun-worshipping aspect of the Beaker folk, before their beliefs merged with the native religion.

This space clearing ritual is based on the romantic Druid idyll constructed in the modern period, rather than on the accounts of Roman historians, who accorded only a few lines to ancient Druidic practices which were evidently not pleasant.

preparation

You will need to gather several twigs of oak leaves from the ground (they should not be picked from the tree). In winter you can use bare oak twigs. A few sprigs of mistletoe can be added if available, but be aware that the white berries are poisonous. Select an "Earth" incense such as sage, pine or patchouli, and candles in Earth colours: black, brown, olive green, mustard-yellow or white. No altar is used in this ritual.

the ritual

Set the twigs and leaves around the space to be cleared. Arrange the incense and candles carefully here and there around the area and light them.

Stand for several moments, breathing in slowly and deeply, with your eyes closed, to

▽ **Stand quietly in the centre of the area, breathing deeply, to calm yourself before beginning the ritual.**

Hedgewitch rituals

The term "hedgewitch" describes a magical practitioner who works alone and very much according to individual style and belief. In days of old, the hedgewitch would have been called upon regularly to assist in house blessings and clearings, in the protection of property and personal possessions, and also to act as an oracle to discover the reasons behind any problems and hindrances. Traditionally, he or she would have lived on the edge of the community, surrounded by hedgerows and perhaps also concealed behind the garden hedge around the house.

Living in harmony with nature, hedgewitches use their knowledge of herbs,

▽ **Hedgewitches have a very close link to the spirit world, and to elementals like the fairies.**

flowers, roots and leaves to make up concoctions for such purposes as healing, protection or fertility. A hedgewitch is able to keep one foot in the material world and the other in the world of spirit, and this is what the hedge represents: the veil between the worlds. The hedgewitch might use any of the following for space clearing.

spirits of place

Everything in the world is made up of energy and this includes the energy that makes up the blueprint for the home and place of work. For the purposes of communicating with them, the various energies around us can be called spirits of place. By communing regularly with the spirits of place, the hedgewitch can discover what is causing particular problems to arise.

fairies and elementals

A hedgewitch believes strongly in the elemental energies that inhabit gardens, plants and other natural objects. These entities are a vital part of the energetic life force system, and together are known as elementals because they are related to the four elements, and each shares the characteristics of the element to which it is related. They are called sylphs (those that are related to the Air element), salamanders (those that are related to Fire), undines (related to Water) and gnomes (related to Earth). Fairies and dryads are nature spirits and the hedgewitch will work with both elementals and nature spirits when seeking causes of inbalance.

Creating an elemental area will provide these helpful spirits with a space to be close to you and will be somewhere you can connect with them at times when you need their assistance. At first you may not believe in them, but once you have made an elemental space and asked for their assistance, you will find that something will happen that will definitely shift your belief towards their existence.

△ **Obsidian, onyx, flint and other dark stones are frequently used by hedgewitches for their rituals and charms.**

dark crystals and stones

Any dark stone can be programmed to draw in negative vibrations from its local environment. Placing dark stones in a problem area can help to cleanse it before it is filled with symbols and objects of warmth and light.

Flint is commonly found throughout most of the world and this stone is a powerful protector against psychic or negative intrusions.

sharp objects

To give protection against negative influences, place needles, pins, thorns, prickles, or any other sharp objects in a jar, then fill it with a mixture of protective herbs. The jar should then be sealed and left in the area that seems to be causing problems. It can also be placed under the bed for protection at night. Putting rusty iron nails around your property, facing away

from the walls, is another traditional means of protection, and will guard against any kind of opposition.

a horseshoe

An iron horseshoe should be displayed with its horns facing to the left in the shape of a crescent moon. Iron is the metal of Mars – the planet of power, strength and courage. A horseshoe placed in this way displays the properties of Mars and moon goddesses.

spells, charms and amulets

Charms such as runic symbols, or those made specifically for an individual, can be used for protection, as well as natural amulets

▽ Hedgewitches display a horseshoe on its side, with its horns facing left like the crescent moon, to invoke the power of moon goddesses.

△ Hedgewitches will often grow and harvest their own herbs, for use both in rituals and charms and for healing.

like oak leaves, onion and nettle. A protection spell is one of the skills sought from a hedgewitch.

herbs and spices

The hedgewitch frequently uses herbs and spices in her work and those commonly used in space clearing include the following:

Angelica: an all-round protective plant.
Asafoetida: removes all negativity, but smells acrid, so is used only in severe cases.
Cactus: all spiny plants and tree branches offer protection. Prickly plants or stems in the home or workplace will deflect negativity from the surrounding area.
Fumitory: to expel negative thought forms.
Garlic: the strong smell and taste of garlic deters negativity. Cloves of peeled garlic can be strung over door frames, or placed in strategic positions and replaced once a week with fresh cloves.
Rowan: all parts of the rowan tree have magical protective properties. String the leaves and berries into a garland and place them around whatever you wish to gain protection for, keeping it out of reach of small children or babies.
Yarrow: a powerful psychic protector.
Salt: central to many of the hedgewitch's practices, salt is one of the sacred items for all magical practitioners. It is a crystal and its cleansing powers mean that it is held in great respect.

A HEDGEWITCH SALT CLEANSING

This ritual can be performed once a week to keep your home or workplace clear and clean. Sweep up any old salt and take it outside your property boundary before repeating the ritual.

Begin at the doorway and move clockwise around the room. Take a pinch of undyed natural sea or rock salt and sprinkle it in the first corner saying as you do so, "Clean and clear this corner [or window, or fireplace] be, from all that is not good for me." Repeat in all four corners, around the door frames, windows, and fireplace, in the same way.

▽ Salt is absorptive and has been used for centuries as a cleanser.

Space Clearing for Life

Wherever we are, we become aware of an atmosphere that we perceive through our deepest senses. The atmosphere of each place is subtly different from any other and can profoundly influence our mood – sometimes it is uplifting, sometimes it is depressing, sometimes it is merely flat and contains no encouragement or stimulus for the spirit. If you dislike the appearance of a room, you can change it, and the same is true of its atmosphere. Space clearing can make a room feel the way you want it to.

To dispel a negative atmosphere

The "atmosphere" of a place can be experienced by those in it as good or bad, but what exactly is it? In occult terms, an atmosphere is a "thought-form" of a certain type. Just as living creatures may have tiny parasites living on them, the psyche has its own form of parasites that attach themselves to it, and these are referred to by occultists as thought-forms.

Thought-forms can be extremely valuable when a magician deliberately creates them, and they form a major part of magic. Unfortunately, the unco-ordinated and primal regions of the mind (the regions responsible, amongst other things, for our dreams) are just as capable of generating a subconscious thought-form as the controlled regions are of deliberately producing a conscious one.

On the subliminal unconscious level, the mind is very susceptible to the psychic vibrations inherent in a place, or produced by people who have been there before, or even by people living nearby and not actually in the place itself. Such vibrations are received by the subconscious mind, rather like a radio set receiving broadcast messages, and a thought-form is created that reflects the nature of the broadcast – it may be happy, sad, gloomy, cheerful, spooky, holy, welcoming, resentful and so on. In our upper, conscious mind we are not aware of how this information – this feeling – arrived inside us, but we recognize it and describe it as the "atmosphere" of a place.

Any kind of good, positive atmosphere is welcome and wholesome, but we sometimes need to cure a negative, unwholesome one. This can be achieved in two ways. We can generate a sufficient quantity of positive psychic vibrations and literally blast them into the affected area, like a kind-of "psychic fly-spray", to change the nature of the vibrations emitted (like changing the broadcast signal). This is the process called exorcism, and it requires tremendous psychic strength and control: it is not recommended unless you are an expert. Also, in nearly every case it is unnecessary, like using a sledgehammer to crack a walnut.

The second way is generally much more useful, helpful and simpler: to continue the broadcast analogy, we can re-tune the receiver so that it picks up a better signal – and the "receiver", of course, is ourselves. In other words, we endeavour to change our own state of mind so that the unwelcome vibrations are no longer received. This process helps us to become stronger, more psychically capable, and less vulnerable to negative influences.

Rituals that produce changes inside ourselves – changes of consciousness – need to be approached with care and sensitivity, and they work best when they are kept short and simple, unless you are a fully trained and proficient occultist.

◁ **As you light your central candle, visualize the flame protecting you and your space.**

▷ **The fourfold breath is used to calm and centre yourself before the ritual.**

the ritual

You will need a selection of white candles and tea lights, including one large white candle, and a rattle such as the one described right. Distribute the candles about the floor of the room and light them. Use as many or as few as you feel is appropriate.

Sit on a cushion in the centre of the room. Light the large white candle and place it on the floor directly in front of you. Spend several minutes performing the fourfold breath (breathe in for a count of four, hold for four, breathe out for four, hold for four before taking the next breath). Then pick up your rattle in your right hand and repeat the following in a deep and warning tone:

Pay attention (shake rattle)
Snake is here (shake rattle)
It is true
Snake is coming (shake rattle)
So beware adversary – snake is ready to strike. (shake rattle loudly)

Then repeat the following chant:

Life is love; love is life; let there be an end to strife.
Let the good replace all bad; let love release all spirits sad.

Let my will reveal the power, starting at this present hour,
To enhance the energy, so that I possess the key,
To allow all ills to go, and to let the goodness flow,
Into this place where I now kneel, let love begin all things to heal.

Repeat the chant several times. Visualize all negativity departing from you at great speed, as you chase it away and re-claim what is rightfully yours.

▽ **All kinds of noise will chase away negativity, but the noise of your rattle has the added potency of the power of the rattlesnake.**

MAKING A RATTLE

Rattles can conjure the ominous sounds of the rattlesnake as it warns of its presence by shaking its tail. The rattle when used in ceremony can either summon the energy of snake to protect, or can warn intrusive energies that they should step back and withdraw. You will need an empty aluminium drinks can, some paper, and a handful of dried long grain rice. Remove the ring pull completely, empty the contents, wash and thoroughly dry the aluminium can. Place the can on the paper and draw round the circular base to form a circle the same size. Cut out the circle. Pour the rice grains in through the ring-pull hole. Place the paper circle over the top of the can to cover the ring pull hole and glue in place. Decorate your can as you feel drawn to do. When it is completed, pass your rattle through the smoke of burning sage, calling for the powers of the rattlesnake to enter your shamanic rattle and for snake to help you.

Dedicate your rattle to Sosho (the snake) and to the spirit of life before using it.

To change an atmosphere

Sometimes the atmosphere of a space needs to be changed if its function is to be altered. For example, if a former bedroom, which has acquired a relaxed atmosphere over the years, is changed into a sitting room, psychically sensitive people may feel drowsy when they spend time in the room. If the planning department of a company moves out of an office and the accounts department moves in, employers may wonder why the accounting staff now seem to be spending so much time in earnest discussion. The atmospheres in these spaces are not particularly negative – they are just misplaced echoes of former thought-forms, each with a residual power of subliminal

◁ These objects will help change the masculine atmosphere of a home office – symbolized by a pen – to the gentler atmosphere of a little girl's bedroom – symbolized by the little pink bag.

persuasion, that need to be overwritten by a more appropriate one.

Transmuting one positive atmosphere into another can be done with a ritual in which you begin by focusing on the old atmosphere, and then swing your focus to the new atmosphere, whatever it may be. This could also be described as stamping a new psychic impression upon a place.

CANDLE COLOURS

Use this list to help you choose candles in the most appropriate colour, which will represent the new function of the room and enhance the atmosphere you are seeking to create.

Red: active areas, energy, dynamism.
Orange: creative areas, socializing, a supportive ambience.
Yellow: thought, the mind, offices and places of study and learning.
Green: areas of relaxation, harmony, balance, calm.
Blue: peace, calm, relaxation.
Violet: warmth and relaxation. A combination of blue and pink, it is ideal for areas where both liveliness and rest are required, such as a dining room.
Pink: inspiration, happiness, positivity.
Purple: depth, reflection, authority, contemplation, for areas requiring stillness, depth and meaning, such as a meditation room.
Silver: magic, dreams, the feminine, for changing a very masculine room into a more feminine one.

Gold: prosperity, abundance, the masculine, for changing a feminine room into a more masculine one.
Brown: grounding, practicality, commitment, for an atmosphere that requires stability and reliable energy. Ideal when changing a mentally oriented space to a more practical one, such as a kitchen or utility room.

YOU WILL NEED

4 small tumbled rose quartz crystals
altar
white candle
2–3 candles in a colour that reflects the new usage of the space
small token of the original use of the space
black cloth large enough to cover or contain the token
rose geranium essential oil and burner
small token of the new atmosphere

the ritual

Set up an altar in the middle of the room using appropriate colours to reflect the change you are making. Put the white candle in the centre of the altar with the three coloured candles arranged in a triangle around it. Put everything you are going to use in the ritual on the altar for a few moments, then take the rose quartz crystals and put them in each corner of the room.

Take the object you have chosen to represent the old atmosphere, and place it in the western quarter of the room. Take the object that is representing the new atmosphere of the room and place it in the eastern quarter. Light all the candles. Start the ritual at the east side of the altar, facing west. Take a few deep, calming breaths and say the following:

◁ As you clap your hands, visualize the sounds driving away the old atmosphere of work, business and stressful activity.

△ After removing the old object, bring in the new one and place it in a central position in the room as a focus point for the new energies.

CLAPPING HANDS
Like any loud and sudden noise, clapping the hands serves to alert and charge the atmosphere. It has the effect of startling a room's energies into an awakened and expectant state.

Go! Depart! Begone ye hence! Avaunt I say, this
*   is my will!*
Be ended, finished, changed, transposed,
Leave no disturbing echoes still!

Clap your hands loudly, then take the cloth over to the object in the west and cover it. Return to the altar, but this time stand at the west side facing east, in the opposite direction to the earlier part of the ritual. Say the following:

Now welcome be, now welcome stay, now welcome
*   is for evermore!*
Be started, newborn, fresh, unfurled,
And bring thy presence to the fore!

Go to the object in the east that represents the new atmosphere and bring it reverentially to the altar to place it there. Sit beside the altar and leave the item there for several minutes while you meditate on it. As you do so, absorb the new atmosphere that is emerging in the room and reflect it back at the object.

When you feel this is complete and the atmosphere has been altered, close the ritual by extinguishing the candles. Dismantle the altar and remove the object that represented the old atmosphere from the room. Leave the object that represents the new atmosphere in a prominent position on a windowsill or shelf.

To make a place feel special

When we expect visitors and spend time preparing for their stay, our aim is to make our home feel especially welcoming. If we are holding a dinner party, we take great care both to prepare good food and to provide a jovial atmosphere. It is important to us to provide for our guests' physical comfort, and we are also concerned about doing the equivalent on a psychic level.

There are two key words that relate to making a place feel special, both materially and magically, and these are "pride" and "respect". Without one, we will not feel the other. When both these elements are brought into play, our place – whatever and wherever it may be – will begin to fill with that special atmosphere of sparkle and excitement.

YOU WILL NEED

altar and orange altar cloth
2 orange or gold candles
frankincense incense and charcoal
    burner or essential oil and burner
wand
additional orange candles for dark
    areas
rosewater in small bowl

the ritual

Position the altar so that you will face east when standing before it. Arrange the cloth and the two candles in holders upon it, together with the incense or essential oil burner and the wand. Place the additional candles randomly around the room in the shadowy areas that light does not normally illuminate, and where the candle glow will enhance the richness of the room's appearance. The aim is to achieve a depth of perspective in the room, so try to arrange the candles in a non-linear way. Try to avoid having any two candles at a similar distance from the altar.

Light all the candles, then stand in front of the altar and bow your head. Take several deep and calming breaths. Use the wand to

"draw" a solar hexagram in the air in front of you above the altar. The hexagram, a six-pointed star (identical to the "Star of David") is associated with the zodiac, the planets and the sun. At its centre, "draw" the symbol of the sun: a small circle with a dot in the middle. As you do this, visualize the outline appearing as a line of brilliant golden light. Then in a commanding voice, say:

Let none undo the spell I cast,
For it is well and three times good;
This place is special now at last,
Be it now full understood!

△ Candles randomly arranged in this ritual brighten every corner.

▽ The solar hexagram is a six-rayed star with a representation of the sun in the centre.

▷ When drawing the hexagram visualize its lines as brilliant golden light.

CREATING AN ENTRANCE

In magical terms, the doorway or entrance to a space is symbolic of a new beginning or a journey of discovery and change. It is therefore an ideal setting to affirm the new atmosphere you are calling in, by using decorations to make the place feel special as you enter.

Bead curtains add a sense of mystery and magic.

Foliage, such as rosemary, ivy and laurel, garlanded around a door frame invites protection, fun and harmony into the room.

Flowers and herbs invite connections with the natural world and convey a sense of ease and relaxation.

Fairy lights strung around the doorway create a sense of light and warmth, and invite the fairies into your space.

Images and charms hung over the door attract specific qualities: angels invite blessings, protective deities offer strength and coins invite prosperous exchanges.

Now pick up the bowl of rosewater and, as you walk clockwise around the edge of the room, dip your fingers in the water and then brush your hand over the walls and floor areas. As you do so, say, "Blessed be this boundary". Where there are areas of the room that might be damaged by the rosewater, pass your hand over the walls a little distance away. It is helpful to visualize that the blessing water is creating a sphere of happiness and peace, as you mark out the boundary of the room.

To close the ritual, extinguish all the candles, starting with the furthest away from the altar and ending with the nearest. Give thanks and discard any remaining rosewater into the earth.

▷ As you distribute rosewater around the room concentrate on what you are doing and visualize a sphere of happiness being created.

To give a sense of belonging

To generate a sense of belonging in a space, we need to start off by feeling special there, and then begin to form a strong bond with it. A space clearing ritual performed with this intent first needs to produce a subtle change of consciousness. Then, at a second level, it needs to establish an aura of association connecting us with the place.

As you develop your awareness of the energy in a room you will be able to sense any imbalance that creates a disturbing or unsatisfactory atmosphere. Such imbalance can be defined in terms of the four elements, and you can consider ways in which you could bring each element into the space, by introducing them in ways that are relevant to you personally. First it is necessary to find which element is required, and each imbalance will tend to manifest within you in a distinct way as you spend time in the room.

▽ A bedroom may have everything it needs to be serene and peaceful, but you might still feel that its atmosphere is lacking something.

sensing the need

Calm and centre yourself before entering the room, then go in and sit down in the centre of the floor, or on the most important piece of furniture, such as a bed in a bedroom, or the sofa in a sitting room. Make your body into a complete circuit by putting both feet flat on the floor or surface, with one hand resting on each knee. After about three minutes, turn your hands palm upwards on your knees and begin to sense the area, also taking into account how you normally feel when you are in the room for any length of time. An imbalance of the elements may be indicated by any of the following feelings:

Crowded – compulsive, mentally intense: too much Air.

Forgetful – unable to remember or recall information, absent-minded: too little Air.

Explosive – having difficulty in keeping one's temper, or a compulsion to outdo everyone: too much Fire.

Disempowered – overly meek and submissive: too little Fire.

QUICK FIXES

Elemental imbalances can be quickly corrected by introducing any of the following items into a space:

Air: music, wind chimes, images of air creatures such as birds, lavender fragrance.
Fire: candlelight, gold or orange materials, fire creatures such as the phoenix, lion or dragonfly, frankincense or copal fragrance.
Water: a fountain, water garden, fish-tank or bowl of water, images of water creatures or plants, jasmine fragrance.
Earth: plants, herbs, crystals, images of earth-dwellers such as prairie dogs or badgers, cypress fragrance.

▽ A bowl of water with some jasmine flowers will help to balance a room.

▷ To be able to sense the need of a room, you will want to be calm, relaxed and receptive.

ELEMENTAL BULBS
Once the needs of your environment have been established, you can balance or summon the relevant element into your room by installing a painted and patterned light bulb.

Air: violet circles on a yellow background.
Fire: red flames on a green background.
Water: blue bands on an orange background.
Earth: citrine and russet brown diamonds.

Overwhelmed – being or feeling too emotional: too much Water.

Insensitive – being unfeeling, callous, hurtful or cold: too little Water.

Dull – reluctant to change anything: too much Earth.

Restless – desiring to change things continuously for no reason: too little Earth.

elemental lighting
Install the appropriate elemental light bulb in the room, preferably in the central light fitting, and light some incense of the appropriate fragrance. Breathe deeply, calming the mind. Absorb the atmosphere and the character produced by the colours from the light falling upon the walls of the room. Then repeat one of the following statements, according to the element:

From Air I arise, in Air I live, in Air my kin, to Air I shall return.

From Fire I leap, in Fire I triumph, in Fire my kindred, to Fire I shall return.

From Water I spring, in Water I form, in Water my kingdom, to Water I shall return.

From Earth I come, in Earth I dwell, on Earth my people, to Earth I shall return.

Meditate upon bonding spiritually with your chosen element. Visualize, as appropriate, clouds for Air, gentle flames for Fire, rivulets for Water or roots for Earth stemming from you and twining about the entire area. This will give you a strong feeling of connecting with and belonging intimately to the place, as you become more and more comfortable with the atmosphere you are creating around you with your

ritual. Once you feel that the balance and connection you are seeking in the area have been achieved, remove the bulb and return the lighting in the room to normal.

▽ Let your hands "feel" and sense the area you are intending to balance and clear.

Space clearing for a new beginning

In order to facilitate a new beginning for ourselves, we must first create the space to enable it to materialize in our lives. For this reason, the acknowledgement of endings is highly significant. Our lives follow cycles that are continually changing, evolving and shifting from moment to moment, and nothing in the physical realm remains permanently the same.

In modern society, we have come to fear or abhor most endings, seeing them as associated with failure or as the loss of something we value or want to keep. However, change is not only inevitable but good, and when we are able to let go of things that do not really serve us, or of an experience that has run its course, our lives can open up in very positive ways.

So to attract a new beginning, we must first close the door on that which is ending. This could be a work contract, a relationship, a house move or perhaps grown-up children leaving home; whatever the situation, it is important to create an ending that honours the change, while remaining positive about it. The ceremony can be as simple or elaborate as you wish. The simplest way to honour an ending is to voice the fact in your life and world, and give thanks for what you have experienced as you indicate your intention to let it go and move on to a new beginning.

moving

If you are moving house, cleaning and clearing out naturally become paramount in the process of moving on. After the physical clearing and cleansing has been finished, an ideal way to acknowledge the act spiritually is to sweep the house symbolically with a bundle of birch twigs or a birch broom, imagining each area being purified as you do so. In ancient times, brushwood from the birch tree was used to sweep out the spirits of the old year, preparing the way for the beginning of the new one. Let the house know of your

SYMBOLS OF NEW BEGINNINGS

These are many ways in which you can call for a new beginning, once you have recognized and acknowledged an ending in your life.

• A pair of lodestones placed as a pair in a central area of a room will call for the attraction of a lover.

• If you see shooting stars and comets together in the sky, wishing upon them calls the Sky Father's protection and blessing for any wishes you make.

• The cowrie shell is sacred to the Goddess and empowers wishes for love, friendship and family. Decorate a small pouch with cowrie shells and drop your written wish inside.

• A bowl of seeds (such as sesame, sunflower or pumpkin) with a wish tucked into them, placed on an altar or on the kitchen windowsill, will encourage the growth of whatever you have called for.

• A birch broom propped up beside a doorway will encourage the old to depart and the new to arrive, and will also provide protection for the home.

• Written symbols, such as Beth from the Druidic tree alphabet, or the Greek letter Alpha, will encourage new beginnings. Write them in places of significance, such as over a written wish or trace them in the air in a space where new beginnings are being called for.

• Write a wish on a piece of paper, fold or roll it and place the paper within the cone of a white lily flower, this bloom is sacred to Ostara, the goddess of birth and new life.

• When you are seeking new work or prosperity opportunities, turn silver coins in your pocket on the first night of a new moon to invite growth in your finances.

▷ In Celtic lore, the birch is associated with January, the month dedicated to Janus, the Roman god of new beginnings. Therefore, sweeping with birch twigs symbolizes your call for a new beginning.

△ Sprinkle blessed, or sun charged, water around a room for a new beginning into it. As you do so, focus your mind on what you are doing.

▽ Rosemary is traditionally associated with remembrance and is helpful for rituals that deal with releasing grievances or loss.

intentions in performing this act, and thank it for having been your home. You can also use the birch broom to sweep the new house you are moving into, as a first step to claiming it as your new home. Here it will have the effect of sweeping away the atmosphere created by the previous occupants, creating space for your own spiritual energy.

To prepare your new home for the beginning of your life there, bless it by walking around all the rooms and sprinkling them as you go with drops of water that you have charged with the energy of the sun. This will add vitality and vigour to your new environment.

relationships

At the beginning of a relationship, we want to spend all available time with our new partner. If a parting becomes inevitable, so does our attention to the relationship, which can sometimes end with total silence, resentment and disregard or, conversely, with trauma, abuse and blame. If possible, try to remember the love you once shared, honour each other's differences and accept that your time together has had some value in your lives. If you can achieve this, you will be closing the relationship cycle with love, which will set up the vibration for love to meet your new beginning. It is a question in all cases of starting as you mean to go on.

Space clearing your office

If you have a private office where you can ensure that no one will disturb you, any of the rituals described in this book can be performed in it: you can simply perform one that you find relevant to your needs. However, most people do not have such privacy at work, which can make it awkward to conduct any kind of overt ritual, so an alternative system of conducting a space clearing needs to be employed.

At its purest and most powerful level, magic needs no special equipment or physical actions, including speech; the entire ritual, including all scents, colours and tools, can be imagined through creative visualization. In order to achieve the full-blown magical results of an occult master by this technique, it is necessary to develop and train the mind and willpower so that anything created in the imagination becomes indistinguishable from absolute reality in all respects. However, only a shadow of this ability is required in order to accomplish a practical and effective office space clearing.

preparation

Try to choose a time for the space clearing when you are unlikely to be disturbed. Even though outwardly you will not be doing anything that would raise any eyebrows among your colleagues, you will be better able to concentrate if you are alone.

Before the day you have planned to perform the ritual, obtain a small notepad to form a scrapbook that lends itself to the concept of a silent, mental space clearing. You will also need to collect a number of appropriate images to represent your working environment. These could be taken from magazines and catalogues. Your tools for this ritual will be nothing more complicated than scissors, glue and paper.

the ritual

Cut out the pictures you have collected and use them to assemble a collage, or compound image of the office, by arranging and sticking them together. Remember that it does not need to look like your own office, nor does it need to be artistic or to

△ As offices are usually crowded and busy places, space clearing at work oftens needs to be a private, mental exercise.

scale, or to have perfect perspective. You are simply aiming for a surreal general impression of an office environment, not an accurate reconstruction.

Everyone is familiar with the ancient voodoo practice of sticking pins into a doll that represents someone you don't like. This follows the principle of sympathetic magic: the idea is that the doll and the target become inextricably linked, so that whatever happens to one will transfer itself to the other by association. Though this practice is definitely immoral, sympathetic magic can be employed in a similar way to space clear the office.

Just as the doll is only a rough image of a real person, your office collage need only be an approximation of your actual office.

◁ Create a scrapbook of images that represent your working environment, and use this as a focus for your thoughts.

▷ If a co-worker is causing problems, take a cactus to work and place it between you and the offending party to create a symbolic barrier.

PROTECTION STRATEGIES

Here are some other simple ways to keep your office psychically protected and clear:

• Display some plants and flowers that have protective qualities, such as fern, yarrow and geranium. Put them in waiting rooms and reception areas to reduce any invasive effects upon your space of the energy of visitors.

• Place smoky quartz crystals in the four corners of your office. Cleanse them once a month by soaking them for eight hours in salted spring water. Rinse them thoroughly and before replacing them hold them in your hands while affirming their abilities to continue absorbing stray energies from your office for the month to come.

You can make one collage, or as many versions as you like, until you find an image that you resonate well with. All you now need to do is look at the image you have assembled and, as you concentrate on it, visualize that you are projecting a space clearing energy into the office. This exercise should be repeated several times for maximum effect.

guarding against negativity

There are other things you can do to space clear your office and repel negativity, such as keeping the area clean and free of clutter, just as you would your home. To protect yourself from negativity coming from another worker in your office, take in a cactus and put it between yourself and the offending party.

If when you are at work you feel a sudden vulnerability, try using your mind to project an image of a guardian figure at your office door. This should be someone you feel safe and happy with, who will keep stray energies (or human nuisances) from entering the office. But it is important never to visualize such a guardian as actually taking the offensive against other people, no matter how much they may annoy you. It is a guardian only, not a hostile spirit.

Space clearing on the move

Like space clearing in an office, space clearing "on the move" can be awkward if people who are unsympathetic to spiritual rituals are likely to be present or to arrive on the scene unexpectedly. You may find yourself in a variety of temporary situations where some psychic negativity may make its presence felt and need to be dealt with for your comfort and peace of mind. These could include hotel rooms, holiday accommodation, cars and caravans, as well as public transport: in short, anywhere that you enter for a limited period but cannot conveniently leave if you encounter a negative energy field. While you would probably not become aware of anything negative during a short journey on a bus or in a taxi, a longer journey by air, sea or rail might benefit from space clearing.

A handy ritual based on certain elements of Wicca can fulfil the need for a space

△ Your hotel room might be charming to look at but could have a lingering atmosphere from previous guests that you want to dispel.

clearing whenever you are on the move. It is unobtrusive and very simple, and can easily be performed in a hotel room or even in a crowded train compartment or a car (providing you are not the driver) because everything is carried out in the mind, rather than physically.

The ritual can be done purely as a mental exercise, but an important magical technique that can help greatly when you are doing a mind-working is to visualize yourself actually performing it as a full ritual. This usually takes only a little practice. Try to imagine a "ghost image" of yourself stepping out of your real body, like a double exposure in a film. Visualize your image standing up and saying and doing the things that the physical you is only thinking. The use of this magical double, or doppelganger, is actually an occult method dating back many centuries. In ancient times people believed that a powerful magus was able to send out such a doppelganger that could actually be seen by others who took it for the real person. Such a self-projection was sometimes called a "fetch".

▽ Ships' cabins can seem cramped and impersonal. Use your space clearing skills to claim the space as your own.

▷ **Try using frankincense or lotus joss sticks, which you can easily include in your luggage, to bless your temporary home.**

the ritual

This is a quick and easy method of conducting a space clearing in crowded or cramped conditions. Throughout the ritual, repeat this chant continually in the background of your thoughts:

> *Echo echo Azarak! Echo echo Zomelak!*
> *Echo echo Babalon! Echo echo Zebulon!*

While doing this, imagine a ball of bright blue glowing fire (like the blue part of a hot flame) starting at the centre of your chest and expanding at about the speed at which a party balloon is inflated, until it has filled the whole area with its glow. (If you are visualizing a doppelganger, the glow should emanate from its chest.) This blue ball is begun again and again, repeating its expansion in waves or pulses. As you proceed, the "balloon" of light expands faster each time, until you can do it in time with the chant, so that eventually each three-word phrase covers an expanding blue pulse. Continue this for a few minutes, then stop and relax.

a portable space clearing kit

If you are regularly on the move, it may be a good idea to assemble a portable space clearing kit, to help bring you peace of mind wherever you may be. Include the tools you feel happiest working with, but a good list of items to include would be:

> *small sage smudge stick*
> *frankincense incense sticks*
> *matches*
> *packets of dried herbs such as*
> *rosemary, marjoram and dill seeds*
> *salt*

△ Salt spread on a mirror or other reflective surface can help to absorb negativity sensed in a room and reflect it away into the light.

The smudge stick and frankincense sticks can be used to "clear the air", and the dried herbs can be sprinkled lightly around the edges of a room to act as a circle of protection if you are occupying a place that makes you feel disturbed or restless. A small handful of salt in each corner can be utilized when the room itself feels in need of cleansing or balancing.

◁ You can make up your own portable space clearing kit quite easily, to ensure happy and successful trips.

▽ Remember that charcoal gets very hot, so take a heatproof container in your kit, and check there are no smoke alarms in your room.

Everyday rituals

The purpose of doing regular daily rituals is not so much to provide a space clearing for a specific room, but to enhance and empower yourself, so that you will have a stronger and more stable foundation. This will help you radiate an aura of authority wherever you go. This practice can also be described as "self charging".

an early morning ritual

The following ritual is a simplified adaptation of an ancient magical technique called "invoking by pentagram", by which various energies can be summoned for a multitude of purposes. In this case, you are summoning a fresh charge of personal psychic energy to strengthen your being, calm all atmospheres you may enter and encourage you to appreciate the joy of a new day.

Light your chosen incense or essential oil. Stand facing a window, towards the east (during warm weather this ritual can also be performed outside facing the sun). Take some slow, deep breaths.

When you are calm, make the sign of the pentagram on your body. To do this, touch the fingertips of your right hand to your

▽ As you touch your forehead to begin the pentagram, say clearly and firmly, "I am Spirit!".

forehead and say, "I am Spirit!" Touch the fingertips to your left hip, saying: "I am Earth!" Touch your right shoulder, saying: "I am Water!" Touch your left shoulder, saying: "I am Air!" Touch your right hip, saying: "I am Fire!" Finally, touch your forehead again to complete the figure of the pentagram, saying: "Thus I seal my affirmation." Inhale the fragrance of the incense or oil for a few moments before beginning the new day.

△ Choose an incense depending on the qualities you feel you may need to call on during the day.

WAKE-UP HERBS
For protection and purification: frankincense, juniper
For physical energy and success: cinnamon, carnation, cloves
De-stressers: bergamot, cedar.

a bedtime ritual

To end the day, you can use this specially modified version of a much more elaborate ritual known as the Middle Pillar Exercise. This ritual has its origins in the teachings of the cabbala, an immensely powerful Hebrew magical system that may be more than 3,500 years old.

Before you begin the ritual, calm and centre yourself. Stand facing west – the direction of the setting sun – and for a few moments relate to the sun setting on the horizon, whether it is actually still daylight or already dark.

Imagine a beam of brilliant white light shining down on you from an infinite height. As it touches your head, it transforms your entire body into light-filled glass, like a clear bottle of human shape. As the light courses down through your body, it changes hue, moving through all the colours of the rainbow. As these colours flow down, imagine any dark areas of your body being cleansed by the rainbow light pushing the blackness down and out through the soles of your feet. As it flows out of your feet,

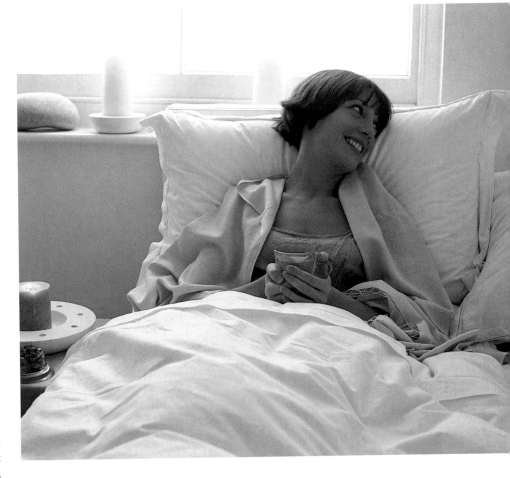

imagine that it is forming a pool or puddle of black mire, and that this pool is then draining away into nothingness, leaving you clean and filled with brilliant, opalescent, rainbow hues.

To add to the effectiveness of the ritual and enhance your ability to sleep, place an amethyst or clear quartz crystal under your pillow before you settle down to sleep.

△ After you have finished your bedtime ritual relax with a cup of dreaming herb tea and allow the tensions of the day to disperse.

▽ Placing an amethyst under your pillow will help you to achieve a deep and untroubled sleep.

A DREAMING TEA MIX

Mix the following herbs to make up a dreaming tea, which can help you to recall your dreams and have a restful night's sleep. (It is not advisable to drink this tea if you are pregnant.)

1 heaped tsp jasmine flowers
1 heaped tsp chamomile flowers
2 sprigs fresh marjoram
a large cup or mug of boiled
    spring water

Place all the herbs in a jug and pour over the boiled spring water. Leave to infuse for 5 minutes, then strain into a cup and sweeten with honey if desired. Sip this relaxing tea about half an hour before you go to sleep.

Space clearing people and objects

As we go about our daily lives, we can pick up energy from our journeys, from those we meet and interact with, from our own feelings, thoughts and emotions and from the environment. The level of demand on our energy will determine how often a clearing may be necessary to counteract the effects of negative energy. For someone who is working with people in a caring capacity, such as a therapist, for example, whose clients may be ill, depressed, or temporarily unbalanced in some way, it will sometimes be necessary to clear at least three times a day, if possible, or after seeing each client. For someone whose existence is more solitary, the need for clearing diminishes proportionately.

The same applies to objects: if they are in regular use a daily cleansing routine could be advisable, but if they are used in less specific ways about once a month would be sufficient. For example, if you are working with a protective crystal during an ongoing dispute with a neighbour, this would be considered "regular" usage and a daily cleansing of the crystal would be appropriate. If you work from home or in a small office and simply wish to use crystals to help keep your working environment

spiritually clean and clear when no particular issue or problem is evident, then cleansing them once a month will probably be sufficient.

There are a variety of ways in which people and possessions can be cleared of negative vibrations. Some of these have been described on previous pages, such as the use of smoke and fire or herbs and aromas. Outlined here are some specific methods that you can use to cleanse yourself or objects around you: simply choose the technique that best suits your circumstances or requirements.

clapping

Creating loud sounds has been a traditional way of space clearing for centuries. You can use this method when there is very little time available and you wish to clear an object such as a crystal, a piece of jewellery or a seating area. Stand in a commanding position, breathe deeply and centre yourself, then clap your hands firmly a few times around and over the object, imagining as you do so that the energies are being commanded to leave and chased away. You may like to make a positive affirmation after clapping, such as, "Be clear, be bright and filled with light."

absorbing

This clearing is ideal when you have been working hard and feel drained or ungrounded, or for an object that has been put to hard use. It can also be useful when life needs to be slowed down a little. Sprinkle some salt on the floor or in a container and stand on it with bare feet, or place the object on top in the centre, for five minutes. During this time visualize all impurities being absorbed into the salt. When the time is up, brush the salt carefully from the soles of your feet (or from the object) sweep it up and discard it in running water. Rinse the salt from your hands and feet and/or the object.

△ When cleansing an object by clapping over it, you should be authoritative and commanding with your gestures.

▽ Laying your bare feet upon rock salt is a good way to ensure that negative vibrations are drawn away from you. Rinse your feet well afterwards.

▽ Objects such as crystals and ritual implements may need daily or monthly cleansing, depending upon how often they are used.

△ **Laying crystals on your body and relaxing for a few minutes will replenish your energy levels.**

crystal cleansing

You can use crystals to clear both objects and people, and this method is most suitable when there is more time available for cleansing. Space clearing yourself will take approximately half an hour, while for objects the ideal time would be overnight or for approximately eight hours. When you are using crystals for cleansing purposes, it is important that they themselves are clean and clear before you use them.

Lie down in a comfortable position and place a smoky quartz crystal beneath your feet with the pointed end facing towards you. Place a clear quartz crystal above your head with the pointed end facing towards you. Place a rose quartz crystal on your chest. Lie quietly for as long as you feel the crystals are having an effect upon you, which should take about 25 minutes. Remove the crystals in reverse order and bury them in the earth for about eight hours before unearthing them and rinsing

them clean. If you do not have a garden, the crystals can be buried in a pot of earth on a windowsill.

To cleanse an object, place it in a dark coloured cloth with a smoky quartz crystal or other black or dark stone such as obsidian. Wrap them up together completely and leave undisturbed overnight. Next morning, remove the object and bury the working crystal in the earth as before.

smudging

Purification using the smoke of smouldering herbs such as sage, thyme and rosemary, is a traditional space clearing method employed by Native Americans. The fragrant smoke has a cleansing effect on the environment, but it is also very useful when you need to clear negativity from a person or object.

You can buy smudge sticks for this purpose, or grow your own herbs and tie the stalks into firm bundles. Simply light the stick, extinguish the flame, and waft the smoke around the object or person to be cleansed. Loose, dried herbs can be burnt and the smoke used in the same way.

▽ **For cleansing with smoke, use a feather and a smudge stick to waft the sweet-smelling herbal smoke around you or an object.**

Correspondence charts

THE SYMBOLISM OF COLOURS

Red: blood, passion, the life essence, power, physical energy, courage, bringing change in difficult circumstances. Associated with Mars, battle, the element of Fire, the south, projective energy.

Pink: love and kindness, reconciliation, peace and harmony, compassion, gentle emotions. Associated with family, children and friendship, receptive energy.

Orange: abundance, fertility, health, joy, attraction, luck. Marks the boundary between the self and others. Associated with the sun, projective energy.

Yellow: communication, the intellect, learning, concentration, also movement, travel and change. Associated with Mercury, the element of Air, the east, projective energy.

Green: the heart and emotions, love, also nature, gardens and growth, money and prosperity, employment. Associated with the Earth element.

Blue: wisdom, patience, possibility, the healing of the spirit, idealism, truth and justice. Associated with the moon, the element of Water, the west.

Purple: royal and priestly colour, a link with the higher dimension, wisdom, inspiration, magic, religion and spiritual strength. Associated with Osiris.

Violet: temperance, spirituality, repentance, transition from life to death.

Brown: Earth and Earth spirits, instinctive wisdom, the natural world. Practical and financial matters, the home, stability, old people, animals. A protective force.

Grey: compromise and adaptability, psychic protection and secrecy.

White: divinity, potential, the life-force, energy, purity. Contains all other colours. Associated with the sun. Helpful for new beginnings, clear vision and originality.

Black: death and regeneration. Conclusions that lead to new beginnings, marking a boundary with the past, banishing and releasing negativity, shedding guilt and regret. Associated with Saturn, the Roman god of limitations, suffering and transformation.

Gold: worldly achievement, wealth, long life and ambition, confidence and understanding. Associated with solar deities.

Silver: dreams, visions, intuition, hidden potential. Associated with the moon and lunar deities.

THE SYMBOLISM OF CRYSTALS

Agate: good for grounding and protection

Amber: good luck stone, draws out disease and clears negativity and depression

Amethyst: peace, protection and spirituality; promotes harmony and balance in the home, clears negativity; disperses electro-magnetic emissions from electrical appliances; heals at all levels; helps with meditation and peaceful sleep, can inspire dreams

Angelite: heals anger, restores harmony, helpful in telepathic communication, connecting with angels and spirits

Aventurine: healing at all levels, dissolves blockages, balances the emotions, green aventurine attracts good fortune and increases perception; pink aventurine heals relationships

Azurite: mental clarity and renewal

Black onyx: protects against negative energy, helps emotional stability, encourages connection with reality

Carnelian: aids creative flow, grounds in the present, inspires confidence, courage and motivation

Chrysocolla: soothes and calms, eases fear and guilt, attracts luck

Chrysoprase: emotionally uplifting, attracts abundance and success, spiritual energy

Citrine: prevents nightmares, enhances self-esteem and mental clarity, brings abundance and material well-being; useful for areas where bookkeeping is done

Clear quartz: amplifies energy, spiritually and emotionally healing and empowering, aids meditation; can be used to dispel negative energy and harmful emissions from electrical appliances

Emerald: physically healing and protective, lends insight and security in love

Garnet: stimulates energy, aids expression, strengthens love and friendship

Hematite: aids concentration, reasoning, memory and self-discipline; healing and protective

Herkimer diamond: releases energy blockages, helps with dream recall

Jade: promotes clarity and wisdom; balances the emotions, facilitates peaceful sleep, attracts prosperity

Jet: lifts depression and wards off nightmares; brings wisdom, health and long life

Lapis lazuli: strengthens will, awareness, integrity in relationships; aids the release of emotional wounds

Malachite: healing, absorbs negativity, stimulates creativity and strengthens intuition; useful for work areas

Moonstone: wishes, intuition and new beginnings; restores harmony in relationships, calms emotions and induces lucid dreaming

Moss agate: connects with earth spirits, brings abundance and self-confidence

Obsidian: place in a room for protection and grounding; dissolves anger and fear; snowflake obsidian has a softer effect, restores balance and clarity

Opal: visionary, attracts inspiration and insight

Pearl: enhances purity, clarity and grace

Peridot: warm and friendly, heals wounded self-esteem

Pyrites: provides protection and defence against negative energies; harnesses creative thinking and practicality

Red jasper: connects with earth energy, emotionally calming

Rhodonite: fosters patience, selflessness

Rose quartz: heals emotional wounds, restores love of self and others; brings peace and calm; can be placed at an entrance to "greet" visitors; keeps the atmosphere positive

Ruby: amplifies emotions, releases and dissolves anger, attracts loyalty, awakens passion and beauty

Rutilated quartz: releases energy blockages

Sapphire: symbolizes peace, gives protection and prophetic wisdom

Smoky quartz: lightly grounding and balancing, counteracts hyperactivity, fosters self-acceptance and awareness of divine protection

Tiger's eye: creates order and harmony, stability, attracts beauty and abundance

Topaz: symbolizes light and warmth, heals and absorbs tension, attracts love and creativity

Tourmaline: grounding, healing and protective, absorbs negativity and brings discernment and vitality; green tourmaline attracts success; pink tourmaline induces peaceful sleep; watermelon tourmaline balances sexual energy; yellow tourmaline increases wisdom and understanding

Turquoise: symbolizes protection, blessing and partnership

Zircon: aids healing and sleep

THE SYMBOLISM OF PLANTS AND HERBS

Angelica: burn dried leaves for protection and healing

Anise: keeps away nightmares

Apple blossom: for love and friendship

Basil: gives protection, repels negativity and brings wealth

Bay: guardian of the house, protection against illness; burn leaves to induce visions

Bergamot: attracts success and prosperity

Blessed thistle: brings spiritual and financial blessings; fresh plant brings strengthening energy to a sickroom

Boneset: drives away evil

Cabbage: brings good luck

Catnip: encourages a psychic bond with cats, attracts luck and happiness

Chamomile: for meditation and relaxation; use in prosperity charms to draw money

Chickweed: for attracting love or maintaining a relationship

Chilli: assures fidelity and love

Cinnamon: aphrodisiac; draws money, protection and success

Clove: banishes hostile or negative forces and helps to gain what is sought; burn in incense to stop others gossiping

Clover: for love and fidelity

Coltsfoot: brings love, wealth and peace

Comfrey: for safety when travelling

Cyclamen: for love and truth

Dandelion: enhances dreams and prophetic power

Eucalyptus: healing and purifying

Fennel: protects from curses: hang round doors and windows

Gardenia: for peace and healing

Garlic: for magical healing, protection and exorcism; especially protective in new homes

Ginger: for success and empowerment

Grape: for fertility and garden magic, attracts money

Hibiscus: attracts love and aids divination and dreams

Honeysuckle: strengthens the memory, helps in letting go of the past

Hops: improves health and induces sleep

Hyacinth: for love and protection

Hyssop: purification; hang up in the home to dispel negativity

Jasmine: brings good fortune in love, friendship and wealth; raises self-esteem; induces lucid dreams

Juniper: calms and brings good health; berries are burned to ward off evil

Lavender: purifying; brings peace and happiness, love and sweet dreams

Lemon: attracts happiness, relieves stress

Lettuce: induces sleep, assists in divination

Lily of the valley: brings peace, harmony and love

Lime: increases energy, encourages loyalty

Lotus: emblem of enlightenment, elevates and protects

Magnolia: assures fidelity

Marigold: enhances visions and dreams, renews personal energy

Mistletoe: for protection, love and visionary ability; hang on the bedpost for beautiful dreams

Mugwort: for clairvoyance, scrying and dream interpretation

Mullein: gives courage, keeps away nightmares

Nettle: wards off curses, allays fear

Olive: brings peace of mind and fidelity in love, fruitfulness and security

Orange: attracts peace, power and luck

Orris: attracts love and romance

Passion flower: fosters friendship; brings peace and understanding

Pennyroyal: increases alertness and brainpower, brings peace between partners

Pine: grounding and cleansing, use for a fresh start

Rice: attracts fertility and money

Rose: blesses love, domestic peace, generosity and beauty

Rosemary: protects the home, brings mental clarity and sharpens memory

Sage: brings wisdom, fertility, healing and long life

St John's wort: burn leaves to cleanse and protect

Strawberry: for love and luck

Sweet pea: for friendship and courage

Thyme: for courage and confidence

Tuberose: for eroticism and romance

Valerian: brings love and harmony, helps fighting couples to find peace

Vervain: attracts money, protection, transforms enemies into friends; brings inner strength and peace

Violet: contentment and love

Willow: use leaves and bark for healing and to empower wishes

GODS AND ANGELS

Agni: Hindu god of fire

Amaterasu: Shinto sun goddess

Aphrodite: Greek goddess of love and beauty

Apollo: Greek god of the sun, medicine and music, patron of the Muses

Arianrhod: Celtic mother goddess, keeper of time and fate

Artemis: Greek goddess of the waxing moon, protector of women

Athene: Greek goddess of war, wisdom and the arts

Auriel: archangel, earth

Bastet: Egyptian goddess of love and fertility, represented with the head of a cat

Brigid: Celtic triple goddess, fire deity and patron of the hearth, healing, prophecy and inspiration

Cassiel: angel who assists with overcoming obstacles

Ceres: Roman goddess of earth and agriculture

Ceridwen: Welsh mother, moon and grain goddess

Cernunnos: The Celtic horned god of fertility

Cybele: Phrygian dark moon goddess who governs nature, wild beasts and dark magic

Demeter: Greek goddess of the earth, corn and vegetation; represents abundance and love

Diana: Roman goddess of hunting and the moon; represents chastity, protects women in childbirth

Epona: Celtic horse-goddess of fertility and healing

Freya: Norse mother goddess of love, marriage and fertility

Gabriel: archangel of the moon, associated with the west

Gaia: primeval Greek earth deity, prophetess of Delphi, goddess of dreams

Ganesha: elephant-headed Hindu god of wisdom and literature, patron of business

Haniel: archangel of divine love and harmony, beauty and the creative arts

Hathor: Egyptian sky-deity, goddess of love, joy and dance, usually represented as a cow

Hecate: three-headed Greek goddess of the waning moon, who rules magic, sorcery, death and the underworld

Hermes: Greek messenger god; represents consciousness, transition and exchange

Hestia: Greek goddess of the hearth and stability

Indra: Hindu god of war; associated with weather

Ishtar: Mesopotamian goddess of sexual love, fertility and war

Isis: Egyptian mother-goddess, wife of Osiris; represents life, loyalty, fertility and magic

Ixchel: Mayan goddess of storms and protector of women in childbirth

Janus: Roman guardian of the entrance and god of transition

Jizo: Japanese protector of children and travellers

Kali: destructive aspect of the Hindu mother-goddess

Kuanyin: Chinese goddess of compassion

Lakshmi: Hindu goddess of abundance, wealth and harmony

Lugh: Celtic sky-god, associated with the arts

Luna: Roman goddess of the full moon

Maat: Egyptian goddess of truth, justice and order

Mercury: Roman messenger god; associated with speech, breath, wind and magic

Michael: archangel of the sun, associated with rulership, marriage, music

Minerva: Roman goddess of wisdom

Mithras: Roman god of light

Nephthys: sister of Isis, guardian of the dead Osiris

Neptune: Roman god of the sea

Osiris: Egyptian god, judge of the dead, husband of Isis; symbolizes regeneration of nature

Pan: Greek horned god of wild things, half man, half animal

Parvati: Hindu mother-goddess, consort of Shiva

Raphael: archangel of the air element, associated with communication and business

Re: Egyptian sun god and creator

Sachiel: angel ruling justice and financial matters

Samael: protective archangel, helps with matters that require courage or perseverance

Selene: Greek goddess of the full moon

Shang Ti: Chinese supreme god

Shiva: Hindu creator god, whose meditation sustains the world

Sophia: divine knowledge and wisdom

Sul: Celtic sun goddess

Sunna: Norse sun goddess

Surya: Hindu sun god

Tara: Tibetan goddess of wisdom and compassion

Thoth: Egyptian god of wisdom and the moon

Tsao-chun: Taoist kitchen god

Uriel: archangel of high magic

Venus: Roman goddess of love and beauty

Vesta: Roman goddess of the hearth

Vishnu: Hindu protector of the world

Zeus: Greek supreme god

Useful suppliers' addresses

UK

Wilde One's
283 Kings Road
London SW3 5EW
Tel: +44 (0)20 7352 9531
Fax: +44 (0)20 7349 0828
Mail order: +44 (0)20 7351 7851
Email: shop@wildeones.com
Website: www.wildeones.com
Sells a wide range of incenses, crystals
and gemstones, and many artefacts from
the Native American culture including
rattles, drums and jewellery.

Windhorse Imports
PO Box 7
Hay-on-Wye
Herefordshire HR3 5SF
Tel: +44 (0)1497 821116
Email: sales@windhorse.co.uk
Authentic and traditional tools, including
drums, incense, offering bowls, prayer
wheels, Tibetan bells, singing bowls and
tingshaws. Available by mail order.

Mysteries
9-11 Monmouth Street
London WC2H 9DA
Tel: +44 (0)20 7240 3688
Email: info@mysteries.co.uk
Website: www.mysteries.co.uk

Tisserand Aromatherapy Products
Newtown Road
Hove
Sussex BN3 7BA

Tel: +44 (0)1273 325666
Website: www.tisserand.com
Essential oils available by mail order.

Sun Essences
English Flower Essence Company
PO Box 728
Norwich NR6 6EX
Email: sunessence@aol.com
Website: www.sun-essences.co.uk
Flower essences available by mail order.

US

Mystic Trader
1334 Pacific Avenue
Forest Grove
Oregon 97116
Tel: 1-800-634-9057 (USA and Canada)
Tel: +1 (503) 357 1566 (from abroad)
Website: www.mystictrader.com
General space clearing supplies available
by mail order.

Nueva Luz
PO Box 31011
Santa Fe
NM 87594
Tel: +1 (505) 986 9163
Email: nuevaluz.com
Website: www.nuevaluz.com
Ceremonial smudging fans.
Lifetree Aromatix
3949 Longbridge Avenue
Sherman Oaks
CA 91423
Aromatic and essential oils available by
mail order.

Alaska Flower Essence Project
PO Box 1369
Tel: 1-800-545-9309 (USA and Canada)
Tel: 1-907-235-2188 (from abroad)
Email: info@alaskaessences.com
Website: www.alaskaessences.com
Flower essences available by mail order,
including specially prepared space
clearing combinations.

Australia

Native Journeys
112 Auburn Road
Hawthorne 3122
Victoria
Tel: +61 (0)3 98 18 88 10
Fax: +61 (0)3 98 18 88 09
Email: nativej@netspace.net.au
Website: www.nativejourneys.com
Handmade drums, rattles, sage, feathers,
resins, tingshaws, Tibetan bells, Native
American flutes, space clearing candles,
essential oils. Call or write for catalogue.

In Essence
3 Abbott Street
Fairfield 3078
Victoria
Tel: +61 (0)3 94 86 96 88
Essential oils available by mail order.

Index